Can God and Caesar Coexist?

Can God
& Caesar Coexist?

Balancing Religious Freedom
and International Law

ROBERT F. DRINAN, S.J.

Yale University Press   New Haven and London

Designed by Nancy Ovedovitz
Set in Minion type by Integrated Publishing Solutions.
Printed in the United States of America.

Library of Congress Cataloging-in-Publication Data

Drinan, Robert F., S.J.
Can God and Caesar coexist? : balancing religious freedom and
international law / Robert F. Drinan, S.J.
       p.   cm.
Includes bibliographical references and index.
ISBN 0-300-10086-8 (alk.paper)

1. Freedom of religion.   2. Freedom of religion (International
law)   I. Title.
K3258.D75 2004
341.4′832—dc22   2004041977

A catalogue record for this book is available from the
British Library.

The paper in this book meets the guidelines for permanence and
durability of the Committee on Production Guidelines for Book
Longevity of the Council on Library Resources.

10 9 8 7 6 5 4 3 2 1

Contents

I

A New Global Right:
Religious Freedom

S cores of constitutions drawn up since the end of World War II have proclaimed religious freedom as one of the most fundamental rights known to humanity. Similarly, international covenants of human rights have exalted the right to religious liberty as a privilege that is so foundational and precious that it should be guaranteed by international law.

Support for the right to practice the religion of one's choice is very new in human history, and it prompts dozens of questions. If the new right to religious freedom were accepted and enforced, for example, would the world be spared the savagery of wars prompted at least in part by the clash of religious beliefs?

The worldwide spread of national and international commitments to religious freedom also begets a host of questions. Can the governmental and other bodies that support this right believe that the absolutism with which most religious bodies have traditionally promulgated their beliefs is now so diminished that the adherents of most religions would not seek to impose their views on others? Is agnosticism now so wide-spread that neither believers nor nonbelievers have the certainty that is necessary to seek to impose their religious views by force? Whether or not this is the case, the origins and implications of these unprecedented world commitments to protect religious freedom deserve intense scrutiny and evaluation.

Support is not universal, and resistance to ensuring religious freedom must also be evaluated. China and India, for example, are not open to witnesses of religions that are not indigenous to those countries. Similarly, the forty or so nations that contain the world's billion Muslims are not always receptive to religious beliefs or bodies whose teachings are, at least in part, contrary to Islam.

In other words, although the vast majority of nations have made a commitment to religious freedom, it is unclear how those nations actually behave in respect to creeds and cults that are at variance with their historic cultural and religious beliefs.

One would like to think that wars inspired by religious zeal were safely in the past. Clearly they are now forbidden by customary international law; after all, the 191 nations that have ratified the United Nations covenants on political and economic rights have solemnly pledged to refrain from such wars. But the international machinery to prevent them is very new and still feeble.

The ultimate reasons why religious freedom is cherished so widely and so deeply today need to be explored and amplified. At its most superficial level, the right to the free exercise of religion is a rule of expediency that can be traced to 1648, when the Peace of Westphalia restored to Lutherans the free practice of their religion in the Holy Roman Empire and extended it to the Calvinists, while recognizing that the dominant religion of a nation normally forms the core of the church-state relationship in that country. Given the presumptive power of the religious majority, religious minorities are protected by the general right to religious freedom. This rule, with some modifications, may be agreeable to the nations of Europe, the United States, and the Commonwealth, but the concept sometimes lacks legs elsewhere.

Of every hundred people on Earth, nearly twenty are Muslim. The fifty-five nations that make up the Islamic Conference are deeply divided over the question of religious freedom. Although most Muslims, if asked, would register disapproval of the Taliban's destruction of Buddhist shrines in Afghanistan in 2001, for example, there is nevertheless a consensus among Muslim nations that the secular state can embrace the full exercise of the rights and duties that derive from the Koran.

The uncertainty around the world concerning the extent to which governments should guarantee religious freedom is one of the major reasons why the United Nations has not pursued a covenant or a legally binding instrument on freedom of religion, as it has done with respect to such issues as the rights of minorities, women, and children. Similarly, that uncertainty is one of the principal reasons why it has never considered establishing a world entity to monitor compliance with the demands of religious freedom, as it has done to implement its covenants on political and economic rights.

As one contemplates the possibility of a world tribunal competent to adjudicate and penalize denials of religious freedom, one must reflect on Christ's predictions that his followers would be persecuted. Indeed, nothing in the New Testament is clearer. Given this received wisdom, why should Christians now seek assurances that they will not be harmed or treated as second-class citizens? In the early years after the Crucifixion, it never entered a Christian's mind—or anyone else's—to insist on the kind of right to religious freedom now set forth solemnly in several documents of the United Nations.

Christians like myself may be asked whether their desire to ensure religious freedom for all who have faith in any religion is at odds with their belief in Christianity. But this suggestion of a conflict of faith is not valid, because central to Christianity is the conviction that no one believes in Christ unless that person receives the grace to believe directly from God. Christ made it clear to his Apostles and to all of us that he chose them, they did not choose him. Faith is not earned or merited; it is a gratuitous gift from God. A Christian may, and indeed must, desire that governments facilitate the rights of all persons who accept the gift of faith as it is offered to them by God.

To be sure, the Catholic Church did not always seek religious freedom for every believer. For centuries the Church held to the conviction that governments should be required to discourage and even ban not only non-Christian religions but any version of Christianity that differed from Catholicism. But in 1965 the Second Vatican Council radically altered that doctrine, so that now the Catholic Church strongly states that any governmental coercion of individuals to adhere or not to adhere to any religion is wrong.

By this policy, Christians seek to protect from persecution not merely themselves but all followers of all the religions of the world. Christians are well aware of Christ's words: "If they persecuted me, they will also persecute you" (John 15:20). The words Christ uttered just before this prediction are equally foreboding: "Because you do not belong to the world, and I have chosen you out of the world, the world hates you" (John 15:17).

People of faith are well aware of the complexity of the

task of guaranteeing religious freedom. The second edition of *World Christian Encyclopedia,* issued in 2001, reports that 84 percent of the world's 6.06 billion persons declare themselves to be adherents of some form of organized religion. Fewer than 2 billion are Christian, and about half of these are Catholic. Muslims number 1.1 billion; Hindus, 812 million; and Buddhists, 359 million. The number of Jews throughout the world is estimated to be 14 million. Animists and others account for most of the rest.

The idea of creating some sort of international legal machinery to resolve clashes between these religious groups may seem quixotic. Indeed, some observers may have thought it unnecessary—but the genocide in Rwanda, resulting partly from religious differences, has gone far to change their minds. But there are alternatives. A unique trial in Belgium of persons who had fled from Rwanda drew on the four universally binding Geneva conventions of 1949 and led to the conviction of Rwandan nationals, including two nuns, in a foreign nation. Some could argue that this approach is preferable to the establishment of a world tribunal. Although the approach used in Belgium may be satisfactory in some ways, however, it by no means ensures uniformity, reliability, or predictability.

Most persons who speak out for religious tolerance may be vulnerable to a claim that they are biased in favor of their own faith. That charge could be made against me, for that matter: the objectivity of a person who by solemn vow is committed to the advancement of the Catholic faith and the interests of the Holy See can be challenged. But as we have seen, the Second Vatican Council made it clear that the Church does not condone any pronouncement or action that allows any shade of "coercion" for the advancement of the Catholic religion. It is certainly clear beyond question that since 1965, the

Catholic Church has repudiated centuries of its customary practices, concluding that no government action that seeks to urge citizens to adhere or not to adhere to any religion may be condoned.

The idea of creating a world tribunal that would guarantee the free exercise of religion will elicit a strong reaction from both believers and nonbelievers. The world has welcomed the pronouncements of the United Nations committees that monitor the implementation of the political and economic rights to which the vast majority of nations have pledged their support. But an international entity sitting in judgment on the way these same nations regard religious freedom raises more serious misgivings, questions, and doubts. The feeling is somehow pervasive that government organizations—or even a transnational legal body—should not get involved in the religious practices of 84 percent of the human race.

But the world also remembers more and more vividly the tragedies brought about in the name of religion by the Crusades, the Inquisition, the persecution of the Jews, and the many wars over religion in Europe and elsewhere. Indeed, the contemplation of such transgressions led Pope John Paul II to apologize for the atrocities for which the Catholic Church can be held partly or wholly responsible.

The 172 nations that participated in the 1993 UN World Conference on Human Rights in Vienna repeated and reinforced the proclamations of world law in favor of religious freedom. But the Vienna Conference made no giant step forward in this area, as the participants felt that the threat to world religious freedom had subsided with the demise of the USSR.

Since then the hindrances to religious freedom in Sudan, Northern Ireland, China, Bosnia, and elsewhere have strengthened the position of those individuals, nongovernmental organizations, and nations that want greater global protection for the right to religious freedom. But the cry for the expansion of this right is not universal. Many people remain leery of the interjection of secular forces—however well-meaning—into the beliefs or doings of religious groups.

Americans generally share a profound distaste for any governmental ruling that could potentially coerce a religious group in what it will or will not do or may proclaim. Although there is no reason that the U.S. example should necessarily serve as a guide for the rest of the world, it does seem to permeate the global debate about what governments can or should do to maximize the religious freedom of persons who are confronted by open hostility because of their religious beliefs or conduct. It is to be hoped that the general international consensus supporting religious freedom will enable the international community to free itself from the vestiges of a past rife with religious persecutions and move toward a future of true religious freedom. The world faces both obstacles and aids as it embarks on this journey.

II

The Dimensions of the Freedom of Religion and of Conscience

In the years since World War II the entire world has repeatedly and insistently proclaimed its determination to maximize religious freedom. The planet's 191 nations have not proposed, much less promulgated, a binding covenant on religious freedom, such as the several covenants on torture, freedom of the press, the rights of women, and the duties owed to refugees. Still, the privileges solemnly proclaimed for religion and its adherents manifest a sincere, worldwide conviction that religion is very special and that society and its laws must give it special deference: it seems to be assumed that law must yield to the dictates of conscience when those dictates are contrary to what the law would otherwise require. Yet this deference to religious freedom seems thin and easily overcome. Terms such as "public order" and "the common good" can swallow even the most imperious claims of religious dissenters.

How can the effectiveness of humanity's announced respect for religious freedom be evaluated? One way is to survey how nations are complying with the demands for religious freedom, some of which have attained the status of customary international law. This test is filled with problems, because certain restrictions on religious freedom and impositions in the name of religion are almost inseparably intertwined with factors of history, culture, and mythology. Another problem is that many nations and several human rights tribunals have tended to avoid clashes between the rights of religious believers and what is perceived to be the common good.

Yet another difficulty derives from the fact that many religious dissenters have not gone to court to litigate their opposition to the law or accepted customs. St. Paul urged Christians to avoid litigation, and many have complied. How many dissident religious groups have bowed to what they conceive to be a restriction on their conscience is unknown and unknowable.

The most important question relates to an ancient issue: whether a nation should or can establish one religion as the official faith of the country. Will world law someday hold that, for the sake of maximizing religious freedom, no nation can formally exalt one religious faith over any other?

Some internationally recognized human rights, such as freedom of speech, freedom of the press, and the ban on torture, have attained such universal acceptance that international law insists that they cannot be annulled or impaired even in times of national crisis. Other human rights, such as the right to a democratic government and the right to religious freedom, combine to suggest that nations cannot tell some of their citizens that, although they are free to practice their religion, they must accept the nation's legal or traditional preference for another faith.

Will international law someday require the Republic of Ireland to delete from its laws the provisions that establish Catholicism as the stated faith of the entire country? Will the exaltation of religious freedom now so clear in international law eventually require Islamic countries to cease to base their civil laws on the Koran, even though the vast majority of their citizens have inherited and presumably accept the Muslim faith? International law has hardly commenced the tricky task of balancing the right of nations to prefer the faith of the majority against the claims of citizens in the religious minority who feel that they have, by law, been relegated to second-class citizenship.

An analysis of the ways in which this task could be approached is much easier in respect to Europe and Latin America than to Africa, Asia, and India. In the past most nations in Europe and Latin America have contributed in one way or another to the world establishment of religions, and several nations, such as Great Britain, retain shreds of this history. The countries of Europe and Latin America could be described as post-Christian. Here adjustment can be made to deemphasize the Christian traditions of the past, with new arrangements extended to immigrants from countries whose ideological makeup does not encompass Christianity.

But all the international declarations on religious freedom insist that each faith must fully enjoy an opportunity to spread its message. Does international law require the governments of Latin America, pervasively Catholic ever since their founding, to offer equal status to foreign evangelical non-Catholic missionaries? Although non-Catholic forces are making notable progress there, resistance is palpable. Here we see the difficulties that accompany the introduction of the full religious freedom proclaimed by international law in nations where a large majority adheres to one religion. What of the right of the Latin American Catholics to be left alone? Surely that desire is no less legitimate for them than the desire of

Africans not to be "involved" by Christian missionaries from countries that once claimed their nations as colonies.

The more one inquires into the proper place of international law in regulating or vindicating religious freedom, the more complex the problem appears. International law has become the norm by which basic human rights are affirmed and sometimes enforced. If international law is to assume a supervisory and enforcing role with regard to religious freedom, should we begin to inquire whether individual sovereign states should look to world law to discover the basic principles governing the place of religion in society?

Many religious groups will be very reluctant even to consider that the place of religion in a nation such as Norway, Nigeria, or Pakistan should be determined by the norms set forth in 1981 in the United Nations Declaration on Religious Freedom. Most of the world's nations would agree, at least in theory, that Article 19 of the Universal Declaration of Human Rights could govern freedom of the press everywhere in the world; this freedom is nearly universally accepted. But when it comes to religious freedom, it is clear that the nations where a religion is a part of the entrenched establishment will not so readily accept outside authorities. Furthermore, in nations with a long-standing relationship between government and religion, many will claim that any weakening of the hegemony of the traditional religious belief would threaten the morality and well-being of the country.

So who would benefit if somehow there emerged an international covenant that regulated the treatment of religious persons and organizations? Groups that would benefit would certainly include nontraditional religions and faiths yet to be born.

It is universally assumed that governments do not create

religions; they come from the depths of the human soul or, if you are a believer in some supernatural force, from a god or some transcendent force. In fact, the mystery of all human existence and the terrible record of governmental abuse make it clear that governments could not be trusted even if a global system to punish governments that violate universally recognized human rights were to be created. Governments are not necessarily the friends of their subjects. Rulers often put their own political fortunes ahead of the rights of those they rule. Only if they rule with the consent of the governed in a functioning democracy will the fear of removal from office theoretically inhibit ruthless politicians from annoying or angering their constituents.

Would the governments of the world be better or worse if religious forces did not exist? Religions assume or assert that they furnish civilizing influences that prompt rulers to treat the governed with respect and kindness. Political leaders sometimes concede this claim, although sometimes, as in Cuba, they don't want churches to be active or even visible. It is generally assumed that the presence of religious faith does make governments more aware of the moral and ethical standards that became embodied in world law when the signatories of the UN Charter solemnly pledged to observe the human rights embodied in the charter and treaties of the United Nations.

What forces are operating to make the United Nations and other global entities more proactive in protecting human rights, particularly religious freedom? Those forces are mostly nongovernmental organizations (NGOs) that were created to protect the rights of such groups as the Christians in southern Sudan and the Kurds. These NGOs have broad constituencies, but there is as yet no worldwide network of organizations united in their efforts to protect the religious freedom of a wide variety of religious nonconformists, dissidents, and conscientious objectors. If there were a global group such as Amnesty International dedicated to religious freedom, the issues would become more clearly defined and the family of nations would develop a consensus on the role of religion around the globe. In fact, the U.S. Commission on International Religious Freedom was designed to do just that, as we shall see in due course.

We are seeking here to resolve questions that have hardly been raised at the international level. In a sense, the family of nations has deliberately set these questions aside as too complex or too difficult to resolve. In the process it has opened itself up to the charge that it has privatized religion by its failure to grant it a place as a juridical entity at some international forum or tribunal. The absence of any real discussion of religious freedom at the world level has also arguably exalted secular moral norms as the only guiding principles for the interpretation and enforcement of international human rights.

The abdication, or at least the silence, of international law on the subject of religious freedom allows nations to feel certain that they will not be punished for doing dreadful things to persons who practice a religious faith of which the government disapproves. Amnesty International and the Human Rights Watch regularly report on the brutal treatment that nations such as China, Bangladesh, and Sudan extend to Christians and other adherents of unapproved faiths. In essence, the world's silence allows that conduct to continue.

In every discussion on human rights—especially on the right to freedom of religion—the unspoken major premise always relates to the question of who is the architect and the enforcer of a society's basic moral principles. Questions related to marriage, education, and the care of the elderly are not is-

sues that throughout history have been resolved by secular societies alone; they have been directed by nongovernmental traditions that claim some authority from a superhuman source.

There is a deep and pervasive conviction among people,
especially in this new age of international human rights, that
governments have committed such incredible atrocities (one
thinks of Germany and Cambodia) that the promoters of universal moral norms should be heeded. The entire movement of
international human rights has reminded the world that governments that follow only the defined demands of their own
leaders can betray humanity, as the dictators and tyrants of
the twentieth century did. This is the fundamental reason why
the architects of the moral revolution that created the new international reign of human rights have consistently sought to
maximize the thrust and scope of religious freedom around
the world.

In the introduction to an impressive 1997 world report
titled *Freedom of Religion and Belief,* its editors, Kevin Boyle
and Juliet Sheen, assert that "there is consensus among those
concerned that freedom of thought, conscience, religion and
belief should be the subject of a new international human
rights convention." But, they say, "it cannot be an immediate
objective." They justify their go-slow policy by citing the work
of the UN special rapporteur on religious freedom, who believes that the best thing to do at the moment is to continue the
work begun by the NGOs in giving priority to religious freedom. Of course, that is not a very satisfactory response to the
countless victims who are suffering because of their religious
beliefs.

The dimensions of religious freedom are profound, complex, and in some ways immeasurable and indefinable. The
way international law defines and treats religious freedom will

almost certainly grow in importance in the years ahead. Indeed, it is not impossible that in the near future one of the central issues in the area of human rights will be the level of attention and enforcement that world law will accord to the boundaries of religious freedom.

The 1981 United Nations Declaration on Religious Freedom is very clear in its assertion that disregard of the right to freedom of religion has "brought, directly or indirectly, wars and great sufferings to humankind." This is especially so, the declaration adds, when the actions "amount to kindling hatred between people and nations."

The abiding antagonism to religion, or at least to Christianity, shown by the officials of the Chinese government may or may not be corrected as the Western world becomes more familiar with China. In any case, many people will remain fearful or uneasy about the influence of religion. The persecutions and wars carried out in the name of religion by nations and factions through the centuries have left millions with the opinion that religions bring more hostility than peace. That impression is widespread and perhaps ineradicable.

Consequently, it may seem surprising that the documents and teachings of international law are so favorable to freedom in the exercise of religion. Almost every international document allows for the exercise of religion in the most generous terms. Only the Convention on the Elimination of Discrimination against Women (CEDAW) is silent on religion; one can conclude that its authors believed that religion through the years has not favored equality for women, and consequently did not expressly urge religious freedom.

The long history of violence and wars associated with religious causes is one of the major reasons there is only a declaration on religious freedom rather than a covenant open to ratification by individual nations. But the deep fear of violating religious freedom has prompted the authors of the international law of human rights to extend rights in this area to persons of conscience and conscientious objectors, especially in the context of war.

Many may feel that any treatment of the evolution of the freedom of religion into a right enshrined in customary international law should not complicate the story by remarking on the international law of human rights that embraces the aspirations of conscience. But the two stories are inseparable. The demands of conscience are included in almost every treatment of religious freedom in the United Nations covenants on human rights.

Guarantees of human rights will continue to be resisted when they encompass acknowledgment of the right to follow one's conscience. One objection is that there are already too many codified rights that lack any meaningful enforcement. Another is the amorphous and subjective nature of the dictates of conscience. A third is the feeling that the problems associated with conscience could or should be placed in the ambit of religious freedom, a concept with relatively definable dimensions.

Although the United Nations Charter mentions human rights in five places, it makes no specific mention of any right to religious freedom based on conscience. The United Nations created the Commission on Human Rights (including members from the United States, the USSR, the United Kingdom, France, and China, along with a dozen smaller nations), and it composed the Universal Declaration of Human Rights (UDHR), which in Article 18 states: "Everyone has the right to freedom of thought, conscience, and religion; this right includes freedom to change his religion or belief, and freedom, either alone or in community with others and in public and in private, to manifest his religion or belief in teaching, practice, worship and observance."

The legislative history of Article 18 is traced in a book by Leonard Hammer, *The International Human Right to Freedom of Conscience*, which makes it clear that the framers wanted to protect not only traditional religious freedom but also "belief," "thought," and "conscience." It is hard to imagine any statement more inclusive.

The complete history of the UDHR leaves no doubt that the framers intended that the right to hold a conscientious belief should attain the status of a protected international human right on a par with the right to hold a religious belief. This right to conscience, new to international law, is, like all of the rights recognized in the UDHR, subject to the limitation in Article 29(2), which states that "in the exercising of human rights and freedoms, everyone shall be subject only to such limitations as are determined by law solely for the purpose of securing due recognition and respect for the rights and freedoms of others and of meeting the just requirements of morality, public order and the general welfare in a democratic society."

It could be argued that Article 29(2) tends to negate the bold claims encouraged by Article 18. But the proclamation of the rights of conscience in a major international document, now a part of customary international law, is an event with enormous consequences.

The language in the UDHR of 1948 was codified in Article 18 of the International Covenant on Cultural and Political Rights (ICCPR). It reads, "Everyone shall have the right to freedom of thought, conscience and religion. This right shall include freedom to have or to adopt a religion or belief of his choice, and freedom, either individually or in community with others and in public or private, to manifest his religion or belief in worship, observance, practice and preaching." The inclusion of the right to freedom of "thought, conscience and religion" in a document now ratified by over 160 nations, including the United States and China, is obviously an event uniquely important in world history.

Also of significance is Article 18(4) of the ICCPR: "The state parties to the present covenant undertake to have respect for the liberty of parents and, when applicable, legal guardians to ensure religious and moral education of their children in conformity with their own convictions." This instinct of parents to provide what they view as appropriate religious and moral education is often drawn from their consciences, but, although 160 nations have recognized it, the right of parents to determine their children's education is largely underdeveloped in international law. At the national level, the right is most common in countries where there is a significant religious or ethnic majority, and parents are accorded the right to send their children to schools consistent with the convictions of the majority.

The protection of "thought, conscience and religion" in the UDHR is echoed in Article 9 of the European Convention on Human Rights (ECHR). The UDHR is the blueprint for the ECHR, although the ECHR provides that the right to conscience may be suspended in times of public emergency. The ECHR also narrows the right of parents to control the education of their children, and some nations, including Greece, Portugal, and Ireland, have entered reservations to Article 9.

The right to conscience is also codified in Article 12 of the American Convention on Human Rights (AmCHR). The authors of this document, coming as they did from largely Catholic nations in Latin America, inserted a right to "profess or

disseminate" rather than merely profess, so a right to proselytize was thereby granted. The Latin American document is also
stronger on the rights of parents. Article 12(4) reads, "Parents
or guardians, as the case may be, have the right to provide for
the religious and moral education of their children or wards
that is in accord with their own convictions."

The Organization of African Unity issued the African
Charter on Human and People's Rights (AfrCHR) in 1981.
That document uses different language to express the rights of
convictions, although in Article 8 "freedom of conscience" is
deemed to be equal to the "profession and free practice of religion." The AfrCHR also stresses the traditional values of the
African community and mandates in Article 27(1) that "every
individual shall have duties towards his family and society, the
state and other legally recognized communities and the international community." Although the approach of Africa to the
definition of human rights is somewhat different from that
taken in Europe and Latin America, it appears that the right to
freedom of conscience is on an equal footing with the freedom
to practice one's religion.

One can conclude, then, that the right to follow one's
conscience has been included in solemn documents of the
United Nations ever since 1948 and that the regional organizations that implement those rights have included the right to
conscience as an integral part of the principles recognized by
the United Nations covenants. Therefore, the right to follow
one's conscience is in international law a largely unexplored
source of very significant personal power. The framers of the
new right to obey one's conscience did narrow it when they
agreed that it did not include an effective right to abstain from
following the law on the basis of one's subjective convictions
of conscience. As suggested later in this chapter, however, per-

sons conscientiously opposed to war may have the right under international law to refuse to make war, with or without a duty to perform alternative service.

Of prime importance to the place of religious freedom in international law is the treatment of the concept in the United Nations Declaration on the Elimination of All Forms of Intolerance and of Discrimination Based on Religion or Belief (reproduced in Appendix A). This declaration, adopted by the UN General Assembly in 1981, is intended to clarify Article 18 of the ICCPR.

Article 1 of the declaration reiterates the content of the UDHR, ICCPR, AmCHR, and AfrCHR in these words: "Everyone shall have the right to freedom of thought, conscience and religion. The right shall include freedom to have a religion or whatever belief of his choice, and freedom, either individually or in community with others and in public or private, to manifest his religion or belief in worship, observance, practice and teaching." Once again, the triad is there—freedom of "thought, conscience and religion."

It is clear that the drafters of the Declaration on Religious Freedom intended to protect conscientious belief to the same extent that religious belief was protected. It is also clear that Article 1 of the declaration was based on Article 18 of the ICCPR and hence was meant to incorporate moral notions more general than transcendental ideas. The authors of the declaration, like the drafters of the UDHR and the ICCPR, avoided any specific language that could weaken the universality of the document.

The authors of the Declaration on Religious Freedom made it very clear to the General Assembly in 1981 that they did not seek the status of a covenant for this document. But the remarkable similarity of the declaration to the UDHR, ICCPR,

and similar documents suggests that the United Nations could
have taken it up as a covenant available for member states to
sign and ratify rather than as a mere declaration lacking any
machinery to monitor or enforce its implementation. But history shows that the right to religious freedom, endorsed and
blessed by everyone in the human rights community though it
be, is not yet ready to become enforceable.

That state of things may have been confirmed by the terrorism inflicted on the United States on September 11, 2001.
Fear of religious extremism was intensified in many Americans on that day; the violence of Osama bin Laden's followers
tended to be generalized to all religious groups. It is easy to
point out that neither the Koran nor any other traditional religious text condones terrorism, but the pervasive feeling is that
Islamic groups, among others, are engaged in a war against the
United States. These feelings will no doubt prove to be another
obstacle to the realization of a true global right to religious
conscience.

Other documents spelling out the right to freedom of
religion include the 1949 Fourth Geneva Convention, which in
Article 27 states that all persons have a right to "their religious
convictions and practices." The 1965 Covenant on the Elimination of All Forms of Racial Discrimination (CERD) also contains familiar words about the right to freedom of "thought,
conscience and religion." The state reports to the UN committee
monitoring compliance with the CERD offer illuminating insights as to how the United Nations commission has ordered
nations such as Zambia, Kuwait, Tunisia, and Burundi to grant
the fullness of religious freedom.

The 1989 Covenant on the Rights of the Child (CRC) also
provides in Article 14 for the "freedom of thought, conscience
and religion." The CRC, now accepted by every nation except

the United States, has developed a working jurisprudence that accepts the rights of parents but accords priority to the rights of the child. The difficult task of the committee monitoring the CRC is to respect, rather than ensure, the right of the child to religious freedom as the child conceives it in collaboration with the parents.

The final document from the United Nations World Conference on Human Rights held in Vienna in June 1993 updates the scope of the right to religious freedom. The Vienna Conference did not, however, expand on the notion of religious freedom, because that meeting was focused primarily on a restatement of human rights after the end of the Cold War.

The evolution in international law of the right to follow one's conscience is a remarkable development. Nothing like it had ever happened before in regulating the sensitive issue of the relationship of the coercive power of government and the prophetic voices of those who are following their conscience. This development is particularly remarkable in that international law has now by clear implication accepted the statements of Martin Luther and Cardinal Newman that the voice of conscience is the voice of God. Consequently, no government can compel a person to act against his or her conscience.

What will be the consequences of this new world law granting the freedom to act on one's "conscience, religion or belief"? For the first time in history there are norms discouraging nations from punishing an individual who acts contrary to law because of a moral conviction derived from conscience. Will it work? Despite all the awful things that have happened to dissidents and conscientious objectors in Cambodia, Rwanda, and the Balkans, one has to hope that a new era has arrived and that governments and organized religion will respond to the new challenges. The challenge is awesome: governments must make provisions for their religious and nonreligious citizens to embrace their right, recognized in international law, to follow their consciences.

Although supporters of this new right based their support on a thousand ideas and ideals, many have been people of faith who nevertheless deplore what religious groups through the centuries have done to dissenters. Such proponents of international human rights, beginning in 1948, changed the world by conferring on conscience a status it had never had before.

The concept is noble, and it has become world law with hardly any dissent along the way. Religious and political leaders, unlike many of their predecessors, have solemnly proclaimed that they will neither reward nor punish citizens because of their faith or their disbelief. Everyone is entitled to follow the path of conscience, whether inspired by religious faith, agnosticism, or personal conviction. Conscience is supreme—subject only to the rational judgment of authorities who must balance this freedom against morality and the common good. All people of conscience can now feel hope and gratitude.

Gratitude rapidly subsides, however, when the question is posed whether the expansion of the rights accorded to the dictates of conscience can furnish some normative directives. Such standards are needed if the world community is to decry the violence of a terrorist angry at a colonial nation or the actions of a Muslim who strikes out at Christians in the belief that the prophet Muhammad would want him to do so. Other examples are plentiful. Does anyone have a right to use violence to curb what he or she conceives to be injustice in Northern Ireland, Israel, or East Timor? One's first instinct is to say that violence to obtain a political objective can never be justified by recourse to "conscience"; but in that case, can passive resistance or civil disobedience be justified even though it causes major disruptions?

While one is rejoicing at the emergence of conscience as a norm in the international law of human rights, one should remember that it is not clear at this time that it offers any immediate resolution of the dicey scenes around the world. The new status of conscience as a norm for judging the validity of human rights, however, may be more useful in the near future than it is at the present moment.

The idea of a person who acts out of conscience often suggests an individual who is out of touch with some realistic standard and who might be inclined to resort to violence. Conscientious objectors, however, may be following the philosophy of Thoreau or the passive resistance of Gandhi. They may not adhere to any organized religion or even have any religious convictions. They may simply be convinced that a situation is wrong and that they must protest in an effort to change things.

Up until the human rights revolution, conscientious objectors had no right under international law to express opposition to a situation they perceived to be an injustice. In some countries, such as the United States, such objectors could demonstrate and hope for the best, relying on freedoms of press, speech, and assembly. Now, however, these individuals possess under international law the right to follow their conscience and use that norm as a defense against arrest and imprisonment.

The amorphousness of the new right predicated on conscience is one of the many reasons why the international human rights community does not have as one of its priorities the elevation of the declaration on religious freedom to the status of an enforceable covenant. But again, the assertion of the right to follow one's conscience is being cited and developed as national courts all over the world contemplate the addition of conscience as a factor to be considered. Human rights activists and theorists are parsing out the good news about the addition of a right to conscience to several norms by which the human rights revolution can be carried around the world.

One would think that the elevation of the idea of conscience to a new and exalted state would redound to the benefit of those persons who are conscientiously opposed to war. People who have come to the truly difficult position of opposing a war in which their country is engaged have to be admired. They are not opposed to the war for political or economic reasons; while they may believe that the war is premature or ill advised, their real objection derives from the conviction that the war is so immoral that they personally cannot participate in it because their conscience will not allow them to do so. This opposition can be even more stark in the case of conscientious objectors to nuclear war, as one of their objections could be the potential illegality of the use of nuclear weapons—an issue that is not free of doubt.

It is difficult to think of a more important claim based on conscience than a conscientious objection to war. It is therefore disappointing that the importance attached to conscience has not resulted in any decisions that have excused conscientious objectors from military service in time of war.

The ICCPR in Article 8 abolishes slavery, but states that "forced or compulsory labor" does not include "any service of a military character" or "any national service required by law of conscientious objectors." An amendment to Article 18 of the ICCPR proposed by the Philippines stated, "Persons who conscientiously object to war as being contrary to their religion shall be exempt from military service." The drafters of the treaty did not accept the amendment, but the legislative history of the ICCPR is not conclusive as to what the drafters found objectionable in the proposed amendment. Some of the founders opposed it as being too specific for a declaration enumerating general principles. Others believed that the right of conscientious objectors to avoid military service should be limited to situations involving the use of lethal force.

In 1987 the United Nations Commission on Human Rights adopted a resolution that appealed to member states to recognize conscientious objection to military service as a legitimate exercise of rights guaranteed by the Universal Declaration of Human Rights and Article 18 of the ICCPR. Twenty-six members of the commission favored the amendment and fourteen abstained. The members who abstained believed that military service should be a duty for represented countries whose constitutions provided for compulsory military service.

Despite the hesitancy of several nations to endorse a right to conscientious objection to war, there does seem to be a developing consensus on this matter. In 1997, 48 states did not recognize any right to avoid compulsory military service on the grounds of conscience, but most of the other 114 nations surveyed did provide a general right not to serve or at least the right to abstain from a combatant role. Perhaps an ideal law could be fashioned after Article 4(3) of the Basic Law of Germany, which provides that "no one shall be forced to perform armed military services against the dictates of his conscience." This law is not so broad as it may appear, however; note that the only exemption it provides is from "armed" military service.

U.S. law is not entirely coherent or satisfactory in its treatment of conscientious opposition to war. At the time of World War I, the Congress accepted a proposal of the Quakers to permit alternative service for men who are opposed to all war because of their adherence to an organized church that espouses passivism. This provision reaches a very small number of conscientious objectors, although the Supreme Court in the 1971 *Gillette* decision expanded the definition of religion to cover spiritual or humanitarian beliefs that take the place of religion in the life of the conscientious objector.

Persons who are conscientiously opposed to a particular tax have an even more difficult time obtaining an exemption than those opposed to war. Taxpayers who seek to withhold a certain amount of their taxes because the money would go to fund a war seldom, if ever, obtain relief. Persons opposed to the use of their taxes for abortions also receive little relief, although the U.S. Supreme Court, in a 5–4 ruling, sustained a federal law that prohibits Medicaid to pay for abortions.

Objections to the use of taxes to pay for war have been rejected in a number of national and international tribunals. The European Commission on Human Rights rejected a claim based on conscientious objection to a particular tax on the grounds that the final destination of the funds cannot be identified. Courts in Australia and Canada arrived at similar conclusions.

The right of conscience is such a new element that lawyers often hesitate to appeal to it for fear that such a claim would indicate that their clients do not have a better legal argument—one based on hard law or religion. Furthermore, such advisers know that decision makers can be skeptical of claims based on the elusive concept of conscience. But as the bard said, conscience doth make cowards of us all. Standards reliant on conscience may begin to look more specific and manageable as organized religion becomes fractionated and the number of persons who adhere to no organized religion increases.

Is it possible that the accumulation of references to conscience in the international covenants and declarations on re-

ligious freedom will give more recognition and credibility to
the consciences of individuals? The sweeping—indeed, the
amazing—surge in the references to conscience as a source for
normative guidelines has to produce all sorts of questions
about the future of the concept. It is clear that the guidelines
of an ever-broader matrix of human rights is enough to furnish norms capable of producing the rule of law in the world.
The thought of allowing every plaintiff to give an individual-
ized and self-centered account of his or her conscience is not
reassuring, but the presence of the idea of conscience in all the
basic documents of the human rights revolution may well mean
that a whole new source of law and morality is on the horizon.

Actually, the idea of conscience is rather well known in
the law. *Black's Law Dictionary* defines it as "the sense of right
and wrong inherent in every person by virtue of his existence."
The idea of "good conscience" is defined as the "moral rule
which requires privity, justice and honest dealing between
man and man." The term "unconscionable" is often used in the
law; its meaning, courts have said, is almost self-evident. Conscience is commonly thought to be the "still small voice." One
who violates it is "conscience-stricken"; he or she is contrite,
remorseful, repentant, self-accusing, self-convicting, chastened,
and sorry.

The term "conscience" is not in the U.S. Constitution
or in the United Nations Charter. Its initial appearance in
the UDHR followed by its subsequent use in virtually all the
major UN covenants on human rights is surely one of the most
significant developments in national and international law.
Conscience is an expandable concept, so its recognition in
world law should not be underestimated. Its potential is almost incomprehensible.

A belief in a conscience illuminated by God in the heart and soul of every human being has been an important part of the Judeo-Christian tradition from its very beginning. Catholic theology developed the idea of conscience, although it has sometimes been overshadowed by the concept of authority. The Protestant persuasions, less dependent on ecclesiastical authority, emphasized conscience, but it is still amazing to see the idea of conscience occupy such a central and crucial position in the international law of human rights.

It is easy to discuss the counterpoint to claims offered by persons who rely on conscience. Critics are ready to point out that conscience may be misguided, erroneous, or deluded, and they are right. Many, perhaps most, people could persuade themselves that their conscience is compelling them to do something that, objectively looked at, cannot be justified. But the concept of conscience now permeates and invades the new international law of human rights. It has an exalted place equal to the noble role that religious freedom has always enjoyed in world law. Moreover, moral ideas in the law and elsewhere have a way of expanding their scope, their significance, and their influence. Who knows what the idea of conscience will come to mean in international law over the next twenty years? Of course, no one can know, but it is one of the most exciting and frightening ideas now evolving in a world still adjusting after the collapse of communism, the rise of globalization, and the development of international human rights as the new morality of the global village.

III
Religion in the Structure
of the United Nations

The reverence for religious freedom in all of the documents issued by the international community, both before and after the drafting of the United Nations Charter, has been astonishing. The right to worship God has now been granted a place equal to, if not superior to, the high place given to the right to a free press, the right to vote, and the right to due process in criminal proceedings.

Despite the massive secularization of society that has been developing since around 1850, the United Nations, reflecting on the genocide of the Jews during World War II, recognized the need to try to prevent such an event from ever happening again. In a sense, the primary purpose of the United Nations was to guarantee religious freedom in order to forestall anything approaching the Holocaust.

Still, the teachings of international law in the century before 1945 drew little from religion. Despite the historic influence shared by religion and international law in the development of Europe, the bonds between the two had become less articulated and observed in the decades before World War II.

As a result, the drafters of the United Nations Charter sought to construct a document that would prevent the decimation of any religious group while simultaneously denying to any religious group the power to reinsert itself as a moral or philosophical power in Europe or elsewhere.

The framers of the United Nations Charter agreed that the document would be neither theistic nor nontheistic. It would go beyond the protection given by the League of Nations to religious minorities, but it would not assert a divine origin of human rights. A slight exception occurs in Article 2, which states that the purpose of the United Nations is "promoting and encouraging respect for human rights and for fundamental freedoms for all without distinction as to race, sex, language, or religion." This is the only specific mention of religion in the United Nations Charter, although Article 1 does assert that it seeks to develop "friendly relations among nations."

Unlike the League, which did not emphasize human rights, the United Nations Charter mentions human rights in four places. Articles 55 and 56 state that all signatory nations pledge to implement the human rights and fundamental freedoms that are so central to the charter and the character of the United Nations. If some observers of the UN Charter are disappointed that it is not more explicit about religious freedom, it should be noted that both China and the Soviet Union were among its founders. China had not yet fallen to Mao's Communist forces, but the Soviet Union was living under a Communist regime. It is therefore quite remarkable that human rights are asserted in the UN Charter as forcefully as they are.

The authors of the UN Charter made it clear that the protection of religious freedom was the central purpose of the United Nations. On June 21, 1946, the UN Economic and Social Council established the Commission on Human Rights.

From the beginning, the commission had the explicit power to establish a subcommission to prevent "discrimination on the grounds of race, sex, language or religion."

But the forty-eight nations that agreed to the Universal Declaration of Human Rights in 1948 were fulsome in their vindication of religious freedom. Article 18 is sweeping: "Everyone has the right to freedom of thought, conscience and religion; this right includes the right to change his religion or belief and freedom, either alone, or in community with others, and in public or in private, to manifest his religion or belief in teaching, practice, worship, and observance." This proclamation was designed to include protection for every person of every denomination in every country.

The statement of the right to change one's religion was the most controversial. It was included despite the fact that the long-held belief of Muslims, possibly derived from the Koran, is that no Muslim has a right to convert to another faith. Because of the inclusion of this right, Saudi Arabia, along with other Islamic countries, abstained on the final vote of approval for the Universal Declaration of Human Rights. The vote of the commission was 27 to 5, with 12 abstentions.

Article 26(3) of the Universal Declaration could be even more important than Article 18 with regard to religious freedom. It asserts that "parents have a prior right to choose the kind of education that shall be given to their children." This assertion of parental rights in education follows Article 26(2), which stipulates that education "shall promote understanding, tolerance and friendship among all nations, racial or religious groups."

The rights guaranteed in Article 26 have been asserted by parents and religious groups throughout the world. Although it is true that the right of parents to influence the orientation of the school their children must attend has not been fully granted in the United States, the implications of Article 26 continue to be enormous. This article specifically recognizes that one of the essential elements of religious freedom is the right of parents or guardians to influence the religious aspects of the schools that the government requires their children to attend. Several cases brought before the European Court of Human Rights have involved Article 26 in combination with Article 18. The decisions seem to suggest that the European Court of Human Rights has not, at least in the opinions of some plaintiffs, fully upheld the right to religious freedom contemplated by the Universal Declaration of Human Rights as well as the Covenant of the European Court of Human Rights.

Article 18, reinforced by Article 26, bestows on religion rights beyond freedom of speech or freedom of the press. The privilege includes the "right to freedom of thought, conscience and religion"—and religion includes belief. The legislative history of Article 18 makes it clear that the freedom to believe and to manifest one's beliefs, "alone or in community with others," is one of the central claims that both believers and nonbelievers possess.

The Universal Declaration of Human Rights assumed that covenants on human rights would be forthcoming from the United Nations or its subdivisions. A major covenant to enhance both political and economic rights was drawn up, but it was necessarily affected by the Soviet Union's seizure of Eastern Europe and the subsequent Cold War. The USSR refused to grant political rights, and the United States was reluctant to guarantee economic rights. The impasse was a devastating blow to the development of human rights in the world. In 1966 the impasse was compromised by the creation of the International Covenant on Cultural and Political Rights (ICCPR) and the International Covenant on Economic, Social, and Cultural Rights (ICESCR). In 1976 both of these treaties entered into effect. Both are strong on recognizing religious freedom, but the free exercise of religion has not really flowered under either treaty.

Article 13(1) of the ICESCR addresses the need to ensure "understanding, tolerance and friendship among all religious groups." Paragraph 3 of the same article refers to the liberty of parents to ensure the religious and moral education of their children in conformity with their convictions. Article 2(4) forbids discrimination of any kind, including religious discrimination. However, the implementation of the ICESCR has not been as effective as its framers hoped. The Committee on Economic, Social, and Cultural Rights has not yet contributed what it could and should to the dialogue on religious rights.

The provisions on religious freedom in Article 18 of the ICCPR track closely the wording of the Universal Declaration. It does not expressly mention the right to change one's religion, but the text surely guarantees that right. All forms of coercion are barred, and restrictions on religious freedom are permitted only if they are necessary to protect public safety, order, health, morals, or the fundamental rights and freedoms of others. One should note that national security is not a listed exception; in general, the religious freedom guaranteed in the United Nations documents may not be curtailed in times of emergency.

Article 18(4) of the ICCPR echoes Article 26 of the Universal Declaration of Human Rights in ensuring that parents have a right to have the religious and moral education of their children conform with their own convictions. Other UN documents on human rights witness to a struggle for consensus on the interaction of religion and education. In 1978 the United Nations Human Rights Committee, which monitors compliance with the ICCPR, took the position that Finland could teach the history of religion in public schools so long as it did so in a "neutral and objective way."

The ideas presented in Article 20(2) of the ICCPR were new in international law when that article was adopted in 1966. Seeking to prevent any repetition of the hatred of the Jews preached by the Nazis, the ICCPR provides that "any advocacy of national, racial or religious hatred that constitutes incitement to discrimination, hostility or violence shall be prohibited by law." This mandate clearly requires member states to outlaw all forms of advocacy or conduct that incite to "hatred." This provision does not require intent; any conduct that involves an incitement to hatred based on religion is forbidden. The ban is broad—it outlaws language that constitutes "incitement to discrimination." That discrimination need not include the "hostility or violence" also banned by Article 20(2).

If the provisions of Article 20(2) were enforceable, would religious freedom be enhanced? Theoretically, yes. For centuries, however, governments, religious bodies, and individuals have engaged in speech and conduct designed to arouse hatred against some disfavored religion. It is difficult to determine how effective Article 20(2) has been within the 151 states that are party to the ICCPR.

In its general comments on Article 20, the United Nations Human Rights Committee makes it clear that member states are obliged to adopt legislative measures to conform with the requirements of the ICCPR. The committee asserts that the restrictions on "hate speech" are compatible with Article 19, which guarantees freedom of speech. In ratifying the ICCPR in 1993, the U.S. Senate insisted on reservations that make clear that the United States will adhere to the freedom of speech recognized by the First Amendment of the U.S. Constitution rather than to the restrictions on hate speech required by Article 20(2). Because freedom of speech is considered one of the most important of the liberties enshrined in the U.S. Constitution, hate speech, though ugly, is generally permissible in the United States. The United States, however, does have several laws punishing certain hate speech, and such laws have generally been sustained by U.S. courts.

In 1993 the UN Committee on Human Rights used its power to issue general comments on Article 18 of the ICCPR. The committee took a very broad view of the reach of Article 18, commenting that it prohibits almost every restriction on religion, including denial of the right to enter a seminary. The committee allowed nations to incorporate moral values in their public school curricula but not if such values were derived from a single religious tradition. If a nation has an official state religion, the rights of persons who do not adhere to it must not be impaired. Laws prohibiting blasphemy are not per se forbidden, but nations are required to provide information regarding the impact of these measures.

The UN Human Rights Committee's treatment of complaints about infringements of religious freedom guaranteed under the ICCPR has not exactly been generous. A large number of the cases brought before the committee have concerned conscientious objection to war, and the committee's reaction has been generally negative. Similarly, as we have seen, persons who have objected to paying taxes that could be used to make war have received little relief. The committee often seems to be satisfied to dismiss a claim of infringement upon finding a single legitimate ground for the challenged regulation.

Is it possible that the United Nations Human Rights Committee will in due course become a tribunal where individuals and religious organizations can obtain relief from a denial of their religious rights? The ICCPR provides for an optional protocol that, if agreed to by a nation, grants the citizens of that country the right to appeal to the UN Committee on Human Rights. At least 99 of the 144 signatories to the ICCPR are parties to the protocol, and the nations that have adopted the protocol contain over one billion people. The signatories include such diverse nations as Algeria, Peru, Canada, and Argentina.

Under the optional protocol, individuals must exhaust all available remedies at the local level before seeking relief from the UN committee. The claimant must also carry the burden of refuting the justification of government for the practice involved. No overwhelming victories for religious freedom have occurred in the UN Human Rights Committee, but it is possible that some surprising results might emerge. Any opinion of the committee, however, is not an enforceable court decree—it is only a statement of the committee's interpretation of the obligations owed by a nation under the contours of the treaty that it has signed. Nonetheless, the committee overseeing the ICCPR and its guarantees of religious freedom could be a sleeping giant; if the appropriate case were presented, it could issue a ruling that would raise religious freedom to a height not yet attained in world law.

However, the advocates of religious freedom were not content with the references to religion in the UN Charter, the Universal Declaration of Human Rights, or the ICCPR. In 1965 these advocates found an opportunity to advance their cause. In 1959 and 1960, anti-Semitism had erupted in several places, and the swastika had become almost epidemic. The General Assembly of the United Nations issued a resolution on December 8, 1962, requesting both a covenant and a declaration on religious rights. In 1972, however, the United Nations decided to give priority to the proposed declaration rather than to the proposed covenant. The difficulties inherent in drafting any worldwide resolution on religious freedom caused delays, but in 1981 the United Nations Commission on Human Rights finally completed a declaration (but not a covenant) on religious freedom. The declaration was adopted 33–0, with 5 abstentions. Abstentions came from Communist countries, which objected that the declaration gave insufficient attention or protection to nonbelievers.

The fact that the United Nations took over twenty years to approve its Declaration on the Elimination of All Forms of Intolerance and of Discrimination Based on Religion or Belief gives some idea of the almost intractable nature of government's relation to organized religion. The matter of conversion was one of the most difficult issues faced by the drafters of the declaration on religious freedom. The governments of Iran and Indonesia, among others, managed to keep the right to change one's religion out of the declaration.

The preamble to the Declaration on Religious Freedom hints at the ambivalence that many persons feel with regard to the history of religious conduct: "Considering that the disregard and infringement of human rights and fundamental freedoms, in particular the right to freedom of thought, conscience, religion or whatever belief, have brought, directly or indirectly, wars and great suffering to mankind, especially where they serve as a means of foreign interference in the internal affairs of other states, and amount to kindling hatred between peoples and nations."

The reference to religious bodies is muted, but the preamble clearly reflects the views of countless individuals that some religions kindle hatred. If this is so, why should religious bodies be given almost unrestricted liberty to carry out their objectives?

The answer is in the next sentence: "Considering that religion or belief, for anyone who professes either, is one of the fundamental elements in his conception of life and that freedom of religion or belief should be fully respected and guaranteed." This consideration recognizes and respects the fact that many persons who adhere to a transcendent idea embrace it as one of the "fundamental elements in his conception of life."

The law stands in near awe of a person who adopts a religious idea as his "conception of life." The UN declaration steps back from making any judgment or evaluation of a person who professes "religion or belief" as being "fundamental" to his or her "conception of life." The underlying belief is that government must respect conscience and may not interfere or intervene in the spiritual life of either the believer or the nonbeliever.

This preamble is one of the most significant declarations in all of the literature about human rights. It simply states, without proof or explanation, that every person is sui generis and is therefore entitled to embrace his or her "conception of life" without interference by governments or groups that oppose it.

In pondering the UN Declaration on Religious Freedom, one can see the aspirations and ambiguities of the jurists and human rights activists who since 1945 have tried to protect religious persons while not unleashing zealots who, however sincere, seek to violate the rights of others. Throughout history, apostates and heretics have brought troubles and grief to countless people. Under world law, they have immunity if their views represent the "fundamental elements" of their "conception of life." At the same time, governments are granted powers that appear to be broad enough to permit repression of religious activities deemed to be undesirable. For example, a government can deny privileges to religious individuals or groups if public officials deem that certain restrictions or suppressions are "necessary to protect public safety, order, health or morals or the fundamental rights and freedoms of others."

On the other hand, Article 3 of the declaration states that "discrimination between human beings on the grounds of religion or belief constitutes an affront to human dignity and a disavowal of the principles of the charter of the United Nations." Discrimination on the basis of religion is further described as an "obstacle to friendly and peaceful relations between nations."

The parental rights affirmed in Article 26 of the Universal Declaration are spelled out and amplified in Article 5(2) of the Declaration on Religious Freedom. Children have a right not to be compelled to receive religious instruction against the wishes of their parents. Furthermore, governments are required to put the mandates of the Universal Declaration into local law.

Although there is no official UN committee to monitor compliance with the Declaration on Religious Freedom, the UN Commission on Human Rights has assigned several special rapporteurs to conduct studies and submit reports on compliance. The several reports of these rapporteurs reveal that a majority of the allegations involve the right of religious choice. Other complaints center on religiously oriented persecution and discrimination. Complaints have come from acts of religious intolerance against the Hindu, Christian, and Buddhist minorities in Bangladesh. Persecution against Christians in Bhutan, where Buddhism and Hinduism are the only recognized religions, were brought to the UN committee.

In 1997 the rapporteurs revealed reports from individuals in seventy-seven nations. It was found that there was severe oppression in countries with an official state religion. The rapporteurs also spoke of religious extremists, proselytism, and cults. In many cases, grievances against the government made by particular groups are intertwined with ethnic and political considerations.

Unfortunately, the findings of the rapporteurs are not well publicized. Even if they were, they do not have the authority or the credibility that would be carried by an adequately staffed committee charged with investigating the failures of member nations to live up to the solemn promises they made under Articles 55 and 56 of the UN Charter.

All of the elaborate framework created by the United Nations to enforce human rights assumes that the right to religious freedom is equal in importance to the right to freedom of speech and assembly and the right to be free from discrimination based on race and gender. These latter rights are protected by the UN Covenant against Racial Discrimination and the Covenant on the Elimination of Discrimination against Women (CEDAW), but there is no worldwide mechanism by which persons who feel discriminated against on the basis of religion can even seek a remedy or protest a violation.

As a result, difficult questions arise. Could or should there be some kind of juridical machinery by which a Christian in a Muslim country or a Muslim in a Christian country could appeal for relief for denial of benefits based on his or her religion? If the citizens of nations that are signatories of the ICCPR, the treaty against racial discrimination, or the CEDAW can bring their complaints to a transnational body, why should individuals who feel they are discriminated against on the basis of their religious faith be denied a comparable forum? There is no good answer to that question except that the leaders of the United Nations have for many years concluded or assumed that religion is too volatile, controversial, or unmanageable to be controlled by some global entity. Underlying this theory is some abiding hostility toward religion as a cause of political violence and even war.

Somewhere beneath the ambivalence or quiet hostility to religion in the minds of millions of people is the desire, even the hope, that international law will more and more privatize religion and preclude it from any active role in international affairs. Many international law experts share this hope; they tend to think that the elements of international order and the advancement of human rights will be better off without the influence or voice of religion. They have an abundance of evidence to support their position. On the other hand, the virtue that ordinarily flows from religious people is needed by every government. In the United States and elsewhere, governments depend on the honesty and integrity of vast bodies of citizens. In many cases, those virtues flow from and depend on the patriotism and devotion of citizens who are virtuous as a result of their religious beliefs.

The appeal to virtue in no way demeans persons who are without religious belief—both groups are protected under the covenants on religious freedom. This is the heart of the dilemma that faces every modern government: how can the government encourage people of faith while not discriminating against nonbelievers? How can a government's ever-deepening involvement in the lives of its citizens encourage the citizens of faith to offer their services in the effort to create a good government?

The task is complex, multifaceted, and subtle. The United Nations has, up to now, ruled that a worldwide enforcement of rights that derive from faith is not necessary or feasible. The world community must concede that millions of believers and nonbelievers are being denied equality because of their adherence to or lack of religious faith. This result is clearly unfair and is contrary to the intentions and expectations of the states that formed the United Nations.

Whether the United Nations will eventually raise the protection of religious rights to the level enjoyed by political and economic rights is not clear. It is surely one of the most important of all the tasks facing the international community at this time. However, it does not seem likely that any movement in the foreseeable future will induce the United Nations to put forward a covenant on religious freedom to elevate the aspirations listed in the Declaration on Religious Freedom into a binding contract. Such a covenant would depend centrally on a ban on intolerance—a concept that, unlike discrimination, lacks a specific legal meaning.

In addition, the leaders of the United Nations, along with the UN high commissioner for human rights, are reluctant to tangle with the Islamic member states. There were only six Islamic nations in the United Nations when the Universal Declaration of Human Rights was adopted in 1948. Now there are at least thirty-five.

While the West is now more informed than ever about the world of Islam, many persons in the human rights community do not fully appreciate the fact that for some in the Islamic world the narrowing of national sovereignty is unknown. The authority of the Koran in some nations cannot be subordinate to national or international law.

The protection of religious groups has become an important part of the international documents on human rights. The League of Nations spoke about the protection to be given to religious minorities, and several European countries signed treaties or made declarations about minorities. The League of Nations system guaranteed many religious rights. For example, faith-based organizations were given the right to apply for public funds for religious, educational, and charitable activities.

The emphasis on minorities in the years of the League of Nations subsequently caused the United Nations to emphasize individual rights and the principle of nondiscrimination. This emphasis was taken to a new level in 1992, when the United Nations issued a Declaration on the Rights of Those Belonging to National or Ethnic Religious or Linguistic Minorities. Article 1 of the 1992 declaration supplements and strengthens the other UN declarations on religious freedom and the rights of minorities.

United Nations entities have issued several other assertions on religious freedom. Indeed, international and regional statements have repeated expressions of respect for religious rights almost like a mantra. The moral and institutional forces behind the omnipresence of acknowledgments of religious freedom have probably not been investigated as much as they deserve. One can say without hesitation, however, that there is a permanent determination in the developed and developing nations to proclaim and vindicate the right to the free exercise of religion. The right to religious freedom is never left out of international dialogue and documentation in the new and surging devotion to internationally recognized human rights.

The four widely ratified Geneva conventions of 1949 contain several provisions on religious rights. The documents prohibit any adverse distinctions predicated on religious faith. The Convention on Prisoners of War, for example, protects the exercise of religious duties, attendance at services, the role of chaplains, and the use of facilities for religious exercises.

Some observers note that some provisions of the 1979 CEDAW seem to clash with some religious traditions, and the convention does not resolve these conflicts. CEDAW's text, however, like so many other international documents, actually demonstrates the high priority that the emerging global law on human rights accords to religious freedom.

The 1960 Convention against Discrimination in Education articulated by the United Nations Educational, Scientific, and Cultural Organization (UNESCO) also demonstrates the high regard that international law confers on religious freedom. Under this measure, separate educational systems for religious purposes are permitted. The document makes clear that religious and moral education must be imparted in conformity with the convictions of the children. The 1989 Convention on the Rights of the Child also stresses that education and religion must be in harmony with the interests of the child.

There are other examples. In 1958 the International Labor Organization (ILO) advocated Convention No. 111, which decried any discrimination in employment on the basis of religion. In 1989 the ILO in Convention No. 169 extended its protection to the right of indigenous people to maintain their religious and spiritual values and practices. The 1990 UN Convention on the Protection of Migrant Workers and Their Families also contains provisions guaranteeing the religious rights of such migrants.

Article 12 of the 1969 American Convention on Human Rights reaffirms the supremacy of "the freedom of conscience and of religion." Restrictions that "might impair [a person's] freedom to maintain or change his religion or beliefs" are not allowed. Limitations on religious freedom are permitted only if they are "necessary to protect public safety, order, health, morals or the rights and freedoms of others." Article 12 concludes with the usual guarantees that parents have the right to provide for the religious and moral education of their children.

The 1969 African Charter on Human and People's Rights

asserts in Article 8 that "freedom of conscience, the profession and free practice of religion shall be guaranteed." The proclamation at the end of the 1993 United Nations World Conference on Human Rights held in Vienna summed up the decades of protection for religious freedom in words and affirmations that epitomize all of the vigorous affirmations of religious freedom in UN documents for nearly fifty years.

The Union of European Nations, founded in 1975, was joined by Canada and the United States in its dedication to the preservation of religious freedoms. Once known as the Helsinki countries, the Organization of Security and Cooperation in Europe reiterated in 1990 that the "right to freedom of thought, conscience and religion" must be "consistent with international standards." That requirement will be relevant when we examine the attitudes of Islamic nations and their insistence that the teachings of the Koran supersede the "international standards."

The 1998 Oslo Declaration on the Freedom of Religion and Belief is probably the most comprehensive of the international statements on religious liberty. Convened to commemorate the fiftieth anniversary of the Universal Declaration of Human Rights, the Oslo nations requested the UN Commission for Human Rights to develop a coordinated plan to focus the resources of the United Nations on religious liberty. The delegates called for action on religious freedom from bodies such as UNESCO, the ILO, the United Nations Development Programme, and the United Nations high commissioner for refugees. They also argued that both public and private groups should use their power to build "a culture of tolerance and understanding."

The Oslo statement and indeed all the pleas from human rights groups around the world reveal the hopes and aspirations for an end to wars and discrimination based on religious differences. The Oslo statement is a cry from the heart for the love and peace mandated by every religion.

Despite the valiant efforts of most of the world, manifestations of intolerance and animosity based proximately or ultimately on religious differences are painfully obvious. Clashes of convictions based on religion are often entangled with political, ethnic, and historical differences. Even without religious elements, these factors might well lead to feuds and wars. But the painful fact is that religions, which in everyone's estimation are designed to bring peace, continue to be the sources of conflict and hostility.

Is it an unrealistic dream to think that if the world guaranteed the free exercise of religion, the family of nations could live together in harmony? The dream has always existed, but it is now more attainable than ever before. The world has seen vividly and unforgettably the raw hatred that led to the Holocaust and has responded by organizing a new legal code for the world. The essence of this creed or code is the observance of human rights; at the center of that code is a transcendent respect for the conscience and the religious faith of every person.

The hope and even the expectation of those involved in the revolution of expectations brought on by the United Nations era of human rights is the establishment of a world court to which persons victimized by religious zealots or by nations hostile to religion can appeal for justice. Although the admittedly imperfect record of the European Court of Human Rights is promising, the realization of the dream of an efficient world tribunal to hear claims of religious persecution remains illusory.

IV
Religious Freedom
in the United States

Many observers of religious freedom proclaim that the United States has reached the best accord in the world between government and religion, but this generalization is open to many reservations. First, every nation has its own story and its own traditions, so it is not clear that any conclusion as to the "best" way to handle church-state relations can be universally accepted. Perhaps guidelines could be developed for predominantly Christian nations, but here again each nation has a distinctive history that must today accommodate situations that were unimaginable even a few years ago. Some Americans urge a deemphasis on religion, lest new religious forces disrupt the apparent peace that exists between government and religion in the United States. To others, such a deemphasis seems likely to cause the privatization of religion and an unwanted growth in secularism.

Although many Americans believe that the United States, its constitution, and its legal decisions are the best in the world, few realize that many other nations guarantee economic rights that are not provided for in the statutory or decisional law of the United States. Few Americans know that other countries are also superior in guaranteeing the rights of women and children. The European countries are superior in some respects because their citizens have a right to appeal certain adverse local decisions to the European Court on Human Rights. This tribunal, while not so progressive as many people would like, has made human rights law in Europe more progressive than ever before.

Meanwhile the United States continues to be xenophobic. This instinct, of course, is contrary to the idealism that impelled Presidents Roosevelt and Truman to make the United States the principal architect of the United Nations and the Universal Declaration of Human Rights.

A particular challenge for Americans is determining whether their government has a duty to use the capacity of religiously affiliated organizations to persuade people to obey secular laws and to respect the rights of everyone. Governments do this almost by instinct. Legal codes everywhere punish people who rob, rape, and engage in other behavior that is clearly wrong. But should government encourage religious principles and church-related organizations in the hope of influencing citizens to commit fewer crimes?

Obviously, governments at all levels in the United States have been eager to promote morality in the public schools. Lawmakers and public officials have become extremely concerned about the welfare of schoolchildren as they have seen the number of juvenile delinquents rise, the rate of divorce increased to almost 50 percent of all marriages, and instances of school-related violence soar. Some legislators have proposed that the Ten Commandments be displayed in public schools, that the Bible be read and prayers recited in the classroom, and that some type of religious instruction be integrated into the curricula of the public schools. All of these measures have been deemed unconstitutional by the U.S. Supreme Court.

The rule of the Court is clear: no law can be constitutional if its primary motive or effect is to promote religion. That test, derived from the *Lemon* ruling in 1971, has been followed but not accepted by a significant and possibly growing number of legislators and parents. It is almost impossible to generalize about whether the *Lemon* test has weakened public morality. The test means, in essence, that religion is a private matter and that the government may not allow the lessons of organized religion to be taught in the public schools.

This arrangement is acceptable to and even applauded by millions of Americans. The policy is clearly sensitive to the children of non-Christians and nonbelievers in public schools. But does it mean that the government, in its efforts to promote a good and law-abiding society, must rely on a form of secular morality that is perhaps derived in part from the Bible and organized religion but is now separated from any body that can clarify its principles or guide its growth and adaptation?

There are terms to describe the free-floating morality communicated in the United States' public schools. Some are pejorative. But the two million U.S. public school teachers and their administrators will certainly not concede that they are diminishing the role of religion by not teaching it directly. They communicate moral and spiritual values. These values may ultimately trace their roots to the Judeo-Christian tradition, but they are no less valuable when communicated apart from their origins. It seems fair to say that the vast majority of Americans agree with the teachers. They want their schools to be neutral toward religion, but neutral certainly does not mean value-free.

Some deeply religious people vigorously argue against this view. They reinforce their position on the centrality of religion in education by pointing to the current moral disorder in the United States. They conclude that all governments must cultivate the moral power of religion. If they do not, they aver, wrongdoing of all kinds will flourish.

If the 1981 Universal Declaration on Religious Freedom ever became a covenant and the United States signed and ratified it, the United States, like any other signatory, would have to report periodically to a new United Nations committee. What would such a committee say about the United States? Could it discover that rights protected by such a UN treaty are violated in the United States? The answer is surrounded by ambiguities. Clearly, opinions vary sharply as to the proper place of religion in U.S. public schools. How would the United Nations supervising group contribute to the discussion? That committee would be required to give deference to decisions on church and state handed down by the U.S. Supreme Court, but it might also look to customary international law to try to discern what the international community has concluded about the place of religious freedom in a nation's public schools.

Parents in the United States who are unhappy with the Supreme Court's ban on religion in public schools would have an opportunity to plead their case through a nongovernmental organization before a committee made up of members from a broad variety of nations. The new United Nations body would look to opinions and practices in 191 nations in trying to reach some conclusions. Would the monitoring body conclude that government should not generally bar religious instruction from public schools?

Another set of American parents would be able to plead

their case to the United Nations commission. These would be the parents whose consciences dictate that they send their children to church-related schools. Such parents are denied all but incidental financial aid by the government, and so undertake severe financial sacrifices to follow their beliefs on how their children should be educated. Could this group find some relief at the United Nations committee on religious freedom?

Most Americans would probably disapprove of any international body sitting in judgment on the proper place of religion in U.S. schools. Some of these citizens might well approve of the ratification by the U.S. Senate of the United Nations' International Covenant on Civil and Political Rights (ICCPR) and the periodic review by the United Nations Committee on Human Rights of the United States' compliance with its obligations under the ICCPR. But Americans generally feel deeply that the United States' resolution of the question of the proper relationship between government and religion must be left to the United States alone; and, they might add, their nation has already created the best existing arrangement in the world.

That assertion may or may not be true. But every member state of the United Nations pledges in Articles 55 and 56 of its charter to live up to the international standards for religious freedom set forth in that charter and in its covenants on human rights. Furthermore, by membership in the United Nations, every nation recognizes that some conduct is now forbidden by international law. As a result, the United States must admit the possibility that it might be improperly denying large groups of Americans, whether they are in the minority or the majority, the full religious freedom they are promised in the documents and treaties of the United Nations.

Absent any supervision from the United Nations, one must individually evaluate the compliance of the United States with the required international standards on religious freedom. It is not an easy task, because the United States was established by Protestants, who quite literally created and supervised its legal development from 1630 to about 1930. That legal framework of three centuries is now being challenged on some points, but its basic substructures enjoy wide acceptance. Any organization, sacred or secular, that wants to change the religious foundations of U.S. law in any significant way has mountains to climb. The architecture of church and state in the United States seems unlikely to change in the foreseeable future. At the same time, the First Amendment, designed only to prevent the federal government from establishing any religion, seems somewhat outdated and artificial in a nation made up of 285 million followers of an ever-wider variety of religions.

A suspicion that the present symbiosis between religion and government will be shattered is widespread. The decision in June 2002 by a three-judge panel of federal judges in the Court of Appeals for the Ninth Circuit that the phrase "under God" in the Pledge of Allegiance is unconstitutional provoked an uproar of protest among politicians and constituents. This strong reaction revealed that many Americans did not want the existing balance between government and religion to be upset. Many voters realized that an informal alliance between government and religion gives recognition and aid to religion, and politicians no doubt used the occasion of the court's ruling to put on a show of piety for the electorate. But beyond these personal concerns, one must acknowledge that the tenuous and delicate interrelationship of religion and government remains an important way to promote morality and stability.

Is the traditional linking of religion and government in the United States consistent with a guarantee of religious freedom to all citizens? The U.S. political scene is honeycombed with benefits to religion. The comprehensive tax exemptions for religious groups of all kinds, for example, are amazingly generous. Their advocates point to the broad tax exemptions generally given to a wide variety of nonprofit organizations as justification. But the exemptions for religious groups are broader, because in order to qualify, these groups do not have to perform a secular function, as is generally required of the nonprofits. Such church-related entities as cemeteries, houses of worship, seminaries, and monasteries are immune to taxes, and ordained ministers have tax privileges on the properties where they reside. Seminarians and clergy are exempted from the draft, Christmas has long been proclaimed a national holiday, and many local governmental decisions have caused Sundays to be considered a near-universal day of rest.

All of this generosity to religion imparts certain costs to nonbelievers in the United States. Quite literally, taxes are higher for individuals and most secular organizations in the United States because they must defray the governmental generosity to the countless churches and religious entities that are not required to pay taxes. One of the arguments used by the proponents of curtailing the privileges granted to religion was advanced by Madison and Jefferson: that it is tyranny to force nonbelievers to pay for the benefits conferred by government on religions. If this argument were brought to a new international commission on religious freedom, how would it fare? No one knows, because a world dialogue on the contours of religious freedom has not yet really commenced.

The issues are complex. Competing ideas have to be refined and the ultimate parameters of religious freedom delineated. In the interim, believers and nonbelievers in the United States must face and try to resolve some thorny issues. The discussion should focus, however, on concepts of religious freedom rather than on the calls to cut aid to religion that now dominate it. International law makes the free exercise of religion central in its decisions; this important interest often takes precedence over desired national bans on religious activities. Some people may object to a discussion that subordinates governmental aid to religious freedom, but the close relationship of these potentially conflicting principles has not been fully resolved either in international law or in U.S. law. The perhaps intractable questions include whether prayers should be allowed at public events, whether faith-based schools should receive governmental vouchers, and whether church-related tax-exempt religious organizations should be banned from endorsing political candidates.

Should Prayer Be Allowed at Public Events?

Prayers at public events in the United States have been neither completely allowed nor completely banned. The Supreme Court disallowed prayers and Bible readings in public schools in the early 1960s. The Congress has never approved a constitutional amendment to allow prayers in public schools—even nondenominational prayers (whatever they might be). The Supreme Court has also disallowed prayers at graduations and banned moments of silence at the beginning of the school day. The Court has also forbidden prayers at the beginning of school sporting events, even those recited by students. Invocations to open the day in Congress, however, have been allowed on the grounds that chaplains were hired by the members of the First Congress, who also wrote the First Amendment.

Some elements in U.S. society, most vociferously some Protestant groups, want prayers at public events. Those who desire an invocation as a symbol sometimes recall the words of the late Episcopal bishop James Pike, who reacted to the Supreme Court's ban on prayer by stating that the Court had "deconsecrated the nation." The need for that sort of ceremonial theism or symbolic deism runs deep in the American psyche. Is it a remnant of the origins of a pan-Protestant country or is it a modern appeal to religion that should be permitted by local choice?

Americans who fear that their country is becoming agnostic or pagan cling to every shred of publicly expressed piety. They clearly identify religion as a part of the soul of the United States and therefore hold on to every symbol of their nation's religious heritage. They do not appreciate—perhaps cannot even conceive of the idea—that their nonbelieving neighbors are offended by such expressions of piety and even feel left out at civil events where prayers are recited.

Those who use the concept of religious freedom to justify their preference for prayers at public events should reexamine their argument. Prayer at a public event cannot be viewed simply as an act stemming from inner conscience. It differs from an act of piety performed with coreligionists. To be sure, according to international law, all believers have a right to exercise their religion in public—but not where it offends the religious beliefs of others.

Muslims and Buddhists and their children probably feel awkward when pan-Protestant or pan-Christian prayers are recited at graduation ceremonies. If Muslims someday become a majority in a Michigan community or Buddhists come to outnumber the practitioners of other religions in a California school district, would prayers of these faiths be recited? If allowed, the Buddhist or Muslim parents and their families would probably want to exercise their rights as the faith group in the majority by having public invocations reflect their religion, but Christians and nonbelievers might well object.

In the future, the United Nations may elevate the Declaration on Religious Freedom to a covenant that will be binding on nations that ratify the treaty. If the U.S. president and Senate eventually agreed to this procedure, the people of the United States would have a new source of law. Under the U.S. Constitution, every treaty becomes the "supreme law of the land." Hence Christians, Buddhists, Muslims, Jews, other believers, and nonbelievers would be able to obtain a ruling from an international court as to what world law sets forth as the meaning of religious freedom. The result might not be what one side in the litigation desired, but at least it would be a definitive judgment on a difficult matter balancing the rights of believers and others.

Should Faith-Based Schools Be Eligible to Receive Governmental Vouchers?

Until recently, the issue of school vouchers in the United States centered on Catholic schools, but the recent creation of thousands of schools in the South sponsored by evangelical churches has changed the debate. The question of financing church-related primary and secondary schools is almost certainly the most difficult and abrasive of church-state conundrums in the United States. Believers and nonbelievers may eventually adjust to the presence or absence of prayers at public events, but the possibility of federal and state financing of schools affiliated with churches raises apprehensions and fears unlike any other issue. The topic is unavoidable, however, after the 5–4 Supreme Court ruling in June 2002 that allowed one form

of vouchers to be used so that poor children could go to predominantly Catholic schools.

It would be helpful if international law and United Nations documents offered some guidance on this issue, but none
clearly addresses it. Even if some consensus could be discerned
at the international level, the opponents of financial assistance
to religiously affiliated schools are not likely to modify their position, and their stance has been more or less supported by
Supreme Court decisions since 1947. In 1965, the Congress, in
granting federal aid to all public schools for the first time in
U.S. history, allowed Catholic Church–related schools to receive some aid for remedial and compensatory education. The
assistance was the same as that given to the children in public
schools.

Since this aid was introduced in Title I, some observers
have predicted that it would grow, but it has not done so. But
the core question remains: should parents who disapprove of
the secular atmosphere of public schools receive a tax credit to
support at least the nonreligious aspects of the private religious
schools to which they send their children? Among the organizations that say no are the national public educational associ-
ations, the American Civil Liberties Union, and several important religious groups. The coalition in favor of aid includes a
strong gathering of Catholic leaders and spokespersons for the
evangelical churches.

The new voices in this church-state controversy come
from those who simply want better schools for the 12 million or
so children who must attend underfunded and underachiev-
ing schools. Their cause is worthy. Can they make progress if
they use only the new, narrow validation of vouchers announced by the U.S. Supreme Court? Could the availability of

these vouchers prompt the public school system to create schools truly equal in training and opportunities that poor families will be happy to have their children attend?

The issue of adequate schools for the poor is intertwined in the United States with the African-American community. Schools once attended by white immigrants and their children are now the schools attended by black Americans and new classes of immigrants. By almost every measure, such schools are inferior, and black children are victimized. If some bold political leaders acted to solve the problem, the demand for private schools assisted by vouchers would be diminished.

Many Americans will shrink from any suggestion that there are international standards that could clarify the new dilemmas surrounding the use of school vouchers in the United States. The Universal Declaration of Human Rights in 1948 proclaimed, for the first time in history, that every nation must provide primary education for all children and that it must be free. Does the requirement that it be free imply that parents whose consciences require religion to be integrated into the education of their children have a right not to be financially penalized for adhering to their religious convictions?

In the United States of the 1800s and 1900s, the public or "common" school enjoyed a central place of acceptance and prestige. Catholics were the principal nonusers, joined by some Lutherans, Seventh-Day Adventists, Orthodox Jews, and a few others. By deeply held belief the Adventists have never sought or accepted subsidies for their private schools. If financial aid were available to church-related schools, would the demand for such institutions rise?

Whatever the future holds on this question, the country and the international community will have to face the question of granting the fullness of religious freedom to persons who find the secular atmosphere of the public school unacceptable and even offensive to their religious convictions.

Should Church-Related Tax-Exempt Religious Organizations Be Banned from Endorsing Political Candidates?

Church-related entities in the United States have from time immemorial gratefully accepted their tax-exempt status. Many of them could not operate if they were required to pay real estate taxes on church property. But the understanding between religious organizations and the government has traditionally been that religions would stay out of politics, and thus not endorse political candidates. This understanding has been spelled out in the federal law that allows everyone to give to religious nonprofit entities and deduct the entire gift from taxable income. The U.S. government has treated this understanding seriously: the *Christian Century*, a nondenominational Protestant periodical, lost its tax-exempt status for a time after it endorsed President Lyndon Johnson over Barry Goldwater in the presidential election of 1964.

In 2002 a bill was introduced in the Congress that would ease the ban on participation in politics: tax-exempt religious entities could begin to endorse political candidates. Some conservative church groups are behind the bill. Civil liberties organizations are not in favor of the measure, even though the present scheme of things prevents the churches from fully exercising the right to free speech. In the past, this sensitive issue has been the subject of hardly any litigation or legislation.

The instinct of many observers—both believers and non-believers—is to retain the ban on endorsements of individual candidates by religious bodies. Although discussion on this topic is seldom conclusive, it seems clear that most Americans would probably accept the widespread practice of many black churches of endorsing African-American political candidates.

The ban on endorsing political candidates can be justified as a quid pro quo on nonprofit tax-exempt corporations. However, the measure can have a chilling effect on the speech of marginal religious groups with strong dissident views. No case of this nature has ever been litigated in the U.S. courts, but the issue obviously goes to the very heart of the idea of exercising one's religious freedom to the fullest degree.

Churches are often countercultural. By tradition and creed, religious organizations do not necessarily reflect the consensus of their community. Thus they are expected to be contrarian, to be dissenters and the rivals of the prevailing view. Indeed, the majority of religious organizations in the United States are opposed to many attitudes accepted by the government. The United States' religious bodies were opposed to slavery long before the government abolished it. Similarly, religious groups came out against a Jim Crow society, the war in Vietnam, and the death penalty before the Congress followed suit. In 2002, religious groups were opposed to many of the government's positions on the military, the environment, and the United States' moral obligation to the world's poor.

Granting and guaranteeing religious freedom in its fullness means allowing religious organizations to use the full power of their considerable strength to attempt to fashion national and global societies into cultures compatible with their views of what is good. Can the United States, at the present time, grant to the vast array of its religious groups the right and the power to steer toward their visions, or would mayhem ensue?

Some Americans like to boast that the United States has developed the best church-state arrangement in the world. It is hard to judge the accuracy of such a vast generalization. But it must be pointed out that the United States has traditionally had a remarkably homogeneous population. Now, however, some of the pan-Protestant orientation that dominated the United States for so long is being replaced, and changes—perhaps even substantial ones—will be forthcoming in the next decades. That is why the role of the United States in the development and expansion of religious freedom in the world is so critically important. Whether the United States likes it or not, its jurisprudence about the dimensions of religious freedom will be watched—and possibly followed—by nations whose church-state problems are much more complex than ours. That is one more important reason why the United States in particular should look to the global parameters of religious freedom as set forth in the documents of the United Nations.

U.S. Unilateralism

The absence of any worldwide monitoring of the state of religious freedom prompted certain fundamentalists and evangelical groups in the United States to support the creation of a federal commission to make judgments on how other nations respect religious freedom and to announce that the United States should adjust its foreign policy accordingly. The National Council of Churches, which represents mainline Protestants and some Orthodox Christians, had first opposed this concept, claiming that the United States should not act as a "Lone Ranger" in such a sensitive matter.

But in 1998 the U.S. Congress passed the International Religious Freedom Act (IRFA). The original bill would have required the White House to terminate all aid and even treaty obligations to nations that were found to be persecuting religion. The State Department and many others protested the rigidity and unenforceability of such required economic sanctions. As a result, on October 9, 1998, the Senate unanimously passed a bill that dropped the automatic sanctions. The next day the House of Representatives passed the bill on a voice vote. President Clinton had no alternative but to sign it, which he did on October 27, 1998.

The bill that was finally passed sets out a menu of fifteen options available to the president when a country is found to be punishing or penalizing persons who practice a religion not favored by the government. Because many of the options can be carried out quietly, it is not possible to know what impact, if any, the U.S. policy has had in such nations.

Resentment continues, however, against the "moral watchdog" role imposed on the United States by the IRFA. Some people feel that the United States is seeking to export its separation-of-church-and-state model. Some critics also feel that the criticisms leveled by the United States against other nations do not take into consideration the fact that many nations have for centuries linked their governments with particular religions. Despite such complaints, however, it is hardly conceivable that the IRFA will be repealed any time soon. The institutions that created it in the Congress are still politically powerful; their members embrace a constituency that is strategically crucial to both political parties.

Domestic criticism of the IRFA has been muted because the Congress was so overwhelmingly in favor of it and because its objectives are so laudable. But it is clear that the policies it calls for can be criticized for focusing disproportionately on religious issues of particular concern to the United States, including the difficulties encountered by American missionaries and by adherents to religions that are particularly identified as American. Critics of the IRFA note that this innovation in U.S. foreign policy was created by the Christian right in an effort to create the impression that Christians are the most persecuted religious group in the world.

In carrying out the IRFA's requirements, the Commission on International Religious Freedom examines the situations in some 180 nations, and its reports direct attention not only to religious freedom but to ethnic and tribal differences as well, as in the case of the hostility of the Muslims in northern Sudan to the Christians in the south. Not surprisingly, China is deemed to be the top offender. Sudan also ranks high. The reports of this commission, located in the State Department, have not attracted the attention that the IRFA's sponsors had wanted. Many observers look upon the reports with some skepticism.

The reports produced under the IRFA are based on information that is publicly available, but they combine and distill the information to an instructive form that can sometimes be hostile to violating nations. But the persons who administer the IRFA and produce the sometimes scathing reports are in certain ways immune to criticism. Elected officials are not likely to criticize any group whose sole purpose is to advance religious freedom. Even agnostics have to concede that countries who abuse citizens because of their religious faith are probably lawbreakers in other respects. Americans who believe that the United States should not act unilaterally in the area of human rights guaranteed by world law have to concede that, in the absence of global protection for human rights, intervention is better than no action at all.

Ideally, the United States should have pressed for greater interest by the United Nations in protecting religious liberties via a covenant on religious freedom. Such an international approach could be highly effective. In 1997, for example, China announced that it would finally sign the ICCPR. The UN Committee on Human Rights, which monitors each nation's compliance with the ICCPR, is now in a position to release its findings on the egregious violations of human rights in China. If the United States had concentrated on establishing international machinery to put a spotlight on the repression of religious persons in China, would this have been a more effective method than a U.S. law?

The reports created under IRFA skip over some thorny questions. Does international law require that sovereign nations admit missionaries when it is known that they will proselytize and seek to inculcate beliefs that the host nation considers alien to or even subversive of its culture? Do Christians from the United States have a right under world law to set up churches in non-Christian countries and seek to change their cultures? Christians and some others hope that the answer is yes. Indeed, Christian missionaries could persuasively argue that they have a mission from Christ himself to evangelize, but neither the reports made under the IRFA nor the international law on human rights has touched on that issue.

One has to be sympathetic to the mission of the Commission on International Freedom of Religion. The spontaneous reaction is to be pleased that another organization, in addition to Amnesty International and Freedom House, is looking into violations of religious freedom and recording them. But it must also be noted that the apparent hostility of its reports to the nations surveyed gives them a tone of moral certainty that seems inappropriate in connection with a topic that is so sensitive and complicated. If the United Nations or some other world body ever established a sort of truth commission on religious liberty, would its reports be similar to those of this novel U.S. creation? Surely their tone would be more irenic, hesitant, and understanding and less accusatory and condemnatory.

In assessing the work of the Commission on International Freedom of Religion, we must not forget that religion was widely suppressed in Russia for nearly seventy-five years, and that it still is in China and in other countries where nondemocratic governments manipulate religion for their own political purposes. It may be, as some Christians theorize, that Christians who live and preach the Gospel will, as Christ predicted, be persecuted and even martyred. Nevertheless, every nation must offer the fullest possible protection so that no individual will be required to go against the dictates of her or his conscience. That is the core demand that international law must seek to enforce in every appropriate and available way. It is clear that there are miles to go before anyone can be satisfied that the law of nations is doing all it can to protect the precious right of religious freedom.

In a way, it is surprising that the United States did not establish the Office of International Religious Freedom before 1998. The American passion for religious liberty was at the core of the ideals that won expression in the Declaration of Independence and the Bill of Rights. The United States saw that precious right of religious freedom trampled upon as the Communists took over Eastern Europe after World War II, and its response was to create NATO and wage the Cold War. The U.S.

Congress also created the Voice of America and many other tools in an attempt to rekindle democracy in Eastern Europe. Yet the United States did not commit itself until 1998 to report to the world on the state of religious freedom around the globe. The Congress did, of course, create the Office for Human Rights in the State Department in 1976. The annual reports of that office do include information on the state of religious freedom, but religious freedom is only one among a growing number of areas mandated by the Congress for review.

The initiative in the Congress to create a separate entity in the State Department to monitor religious freedom came, strangely enough, after the USSR had withdrawn from Eastern Europe and the "Evil Empire" had collapsed. The reasons for this unusual phenomenon will be fascinating to discover as history is written. It is clear, however, that the unprecedented emphasis on the free exercise of religion, while treated with suspicion by some observers when it was initiated, has become a respected and appreciated part of U.S. foreign policy.

Some of the 194 nations surveyed in the first annual report on international religious freedom, issued by the Department of State in September 1999, responded with hostility, but many countries and many human rights activists were grateful. IRFA is guided by its own independent bipartisan commission, which in May 2000 issued its own annual report, focusing on three countries of concern—China, Sudan, and Russia.

One basic truth in the interaction of government and religion is that a government should not seek to create the values of the society that it manages. The government should reflect preexisting values on the fundamental issues confronting a society, such as the structure of the family and the nature and hierarchy of crimes. No government may invent its own morality; to do so would not be ruling with the consent of the governed. At the same time, no government can simply accept unilaterally a code of values inherited from the religious traditions of previous generations. Nevertheless, a nation should be slow to abandon laws, practices, and customs rooted in a consensus that derives ultimately from a religious framework.

Many Americans feel that the decline in their nation's morality is due to the reluctance of the U.S. government to enforce traditional religious standards. The government has allowed laws on divorce and abortion to be modified or repealed. It has not enforced other laws related to extramarital sexual relations, pornography, and homosexuality. Rightly or wrongly, many citizens wish that the government and the courts had preserved and perpetuated the basic moral codes that prevailed in the country from 1790 to roughly the 1960s.

But no one can be certain of the origin of the current state of U.S. public morality. Governments cannot continue to abide by moral values ultimately derived from a consensus that is no longer controlling, and it could be argued that such a shift in underlying religious opinion has occurred in the United States. Moreover, many laws that support religion deal with extremely private, consensual conduct, and some people argue that a government should not insist on maintaining laws that have proved to be unenforceable.

All of these factors are weighed by the people who apply the IRFA to the world scene. Understandably, these analysts shy away from the difficult questions, preferring to report on the topic of global religious freedom from a relativistic perspective that reflects the views of very different societies on the place of religion.

The work of the Commission on International Freedom of Religion has been facilitated and made more visible by the near-doubling of the number of democracies in the world during the 1990s. The rebirth of democracy in Eastern Europe has prompted an amazing revival of religious organizations in that region. The commission's reports have related some of the victories for religious freedom in such nations as Poland and Lithuania.

The 2000 annual report produced under the IRFA sets forth the belief that "each religious tradition has a moral code, a way of understanding who we are and how we ought to order our lives together. The articulation of these understandings in the public square is not something to be feared by democracies. Rather it makes a vital contribution to the development of public policy." The rhetoric about preaching in the public square, although familiar in the United States, is not exactly prominent in the language of international law or human rights. But it seems to be a truism that democratic institutions are strengthened by the free expression of religious ideas. Any attempt to apply that assumption to nondemocratic states such as China raises complex problems.

The free exercise of religion is guaranteed in the ICCPR, to which 144 countries are signatories. But the State Department's 2000 report on international religious freedom states that "much of the world's population live in countries in which the right to religious freedom is restricted or prohibited." The report notes that the history and culture of several countries have resulted in policies that give preference "to favored religions while disadvantaging others, in contravention of international standards." Some observers would quarrel with the blanket statement that preferential treatment of one religion is "in contravention of international instruments." But the State Department frowns on any arrangement under which a religious group must register with the state before it can operate. Such an arrangement is by nature, the State Department report implies, subject to local abuse.

The State Department's Commission on International Religious Freedom has brought together in its report a vast amount of information on the state of religious freedom in all but a handful of governments. The commentary reveals that the state of religious freedom in predominantly Islamic nations is mixed and uneven. It is clear that the elected and spiritual leaders of many of these nations desire to keep their countries predominantly Islamic. There are extreme examples, such as Afghanistan, where Muslim leaders destroyed even the symbols of a long-ago Hindu presence.

A reading of the State Department report tends to leave one with a sense that religion is a powerful and sometimes fanatic force. When political leaders set an objective for themselves, they can use or misuse religion to attain it. When religious authorities embrace a sectarian objective, they can manipulate public officials by offering them salvation and even sanctification if they follow their lead.

Countries that have obtained emancipation from colonial powers can have uniquely negative views about the religion of their former colonizers. Muslims in Indonesia, for example, may feel that Dutch colonists harmed their nation's culture and demeaned their Islamic traditions. As a result, they are not likely to be friendly or receptive to any institution that the Dutch imposed on them, including religion.

How should international law prescribe for this situation? Indonesia has pledged to extend religious freedom, as required by the Universal Declaration of Human Rights and the ICCPR. Does this mean that Indonesia cannot impose its Islamic traditions if doing so would relegate the Reformed Church imported by Dutch colonists to second place? The State Department report is not required to raise or resolve this difficult question. It is supposed to report only factual situations as they appear.

A related question awaiting resolution is whether the international law of human rights requires a nation to allow proselytizing. Many believers feel compelled to spread their faith. Can a nation rightly prohibit attempts to convert its citizens, and is the Greek Constitution, which prohibits proselytizing, contrary to the world law on human rights? There is currently no judicial body competent to decide the issue.

In the State Department report on religious freedom one can see the legal and political effects of the centuries of colonialism as well as the footprints of the original indigenous religious traditions of the once-colonized areas. Is a pattern of accommodation developing, or is the situation moving toward religious wars in some parts of the world? One does not even want to raise such a possibility, but the hundred or more post-colonial nations that are being traumatized by globalization can act in unpredictable ways—especially if their religious and political leaders decide to rely on each other to bring about their separate but similar objectives.

Each year, nations that do not have a Christian origin or background will read or hear about the United States' criticisms and even denunciations of the way they treat religious groups. These statements will be seen as the mighty United States telling those countries that they must be religiously pluralistic, that they have to allow sects they deem to be against the public interest, and that they have to treat all religions equally, even though such a notion goes against their traditions and convictions of hundreds of years.

If these pronouncements were instead coming from the United Nations or some other truly international body, they would be more acceptable to some countries and would be less vulnerable to charges of cultural relativity. In addition, a report from a world body would not have the baggage that attaches to an official report of the United States, a nation that tens of millions of people view as the fountainhead of pornography, violent movies, consumerism, and materialism.

Another feature of the State Department's report that is bothersome is its lack of even-handedness. It reports without comment, for example, that the constitution of Malta establishes Catholicism as the state religion, follows Catholic doctrine by banning all divorce, and makes instruction in Catholicism compulsory in all schools. There is no indication in the State Department report that the situation in Malta may be inconsistent with international standards of religious freedom.

The State Department report also notes that even though the Holocaust claimed 200,000 Jews in Lithuania, 10 percent of the population, a "certain level of anti-Semitism persists" there. The question whether international standards of religious freedom demand some form of reparation goes unasked. The report on Slovenia relates that when this tiny country was a part of the Socialist Federal Republic of Yugoslavia, most of the property of the Catholic Church was confiscated and nationalized. Less than one-third of the cases concerning restitution of that property have been concluded. Is this an issue of religious freedom on which the government of Slovenia must comply with the clear standards of justice incorporated in international law?

The report's account of religious freedom in Spain offers more questions and puzzles. Spain's 1978 constitution declares the country to be a secular state, but the Catholics receive more benefits than the country's 350,000 Protestants and 450,000 Muslims. Taxpayers can allocate one-half of 1 percent of their taxes to the Catholic Church, but it was not until the year 2000 that this privilege was finally extended to Protestants and Muslims. Further, Spain's Jewish community continues to request a one-time payment in reparation for the expulsion of the Jews in 1492. Moreover, Spain, like most other European countries, does not like "sects." In 1989 a new law authorized the investigation of some two hundred allegedly "destructive sects" with at least 100,000 members. The perception of "cults" in Europe is explored in greater detail in Chapter 9.

The State Department report notes that officers of U.S. embassies regularly discuss matters of government-religion relations with the leaders of various denominations in the countries where they are stationed. But it is not clear what legal or human rights principles State Department officials use as the basis for their attempts at reconciliation. This is not necessarily a criticism of the State Department, because the appropriate standards by which to judge restrictions on the free exercise of religion are just beginning to be articulated. There are several basic norms, but how they are to be expressed and integrated depends on the context. It is difficult, for example, to resolve the question whether a government may be presumed to have a right to restrict its citizens' activities in order to strengthen public morality, even if such restrictions curb the religious aspirations of some of them.

At first glance, some things look easy. But in seeking a balance between the imperatives of religious traditions and the demands of convenience and common sense, the correct balancing principles to be applied sometimes defy analysis. The traditional expectation that a widow will burn herself to death on the pyre of her husband, the practice of sati in parts of India, would seem to be indefensible. But if the members of the community who practice this custom are convinced that this measure is decreed by a divine power, how can any human authority forbid it in the name of rationality or the rights of women? At least in theory, the provisions for religious freedom in international law hold that people have the right to follow their conscience; no exception is made for conscientious actions that no legal system would allow.

But many experts on the emerging international law of religious freedom would disagree that the practice of burning a widow has to be allowed. They would theorize that legal and political authorities can sometimes use reason and the basic norms of morality to override the conclusions of some equally learned theological or mystical authorities. Such a conclusion, however, invites the dangers of the "slippery slope," the abuses of utilitarianism, and the dangers of consequentialism. It also obscures the fact that many believers have faith that God sometimes intervenes in human affairs with terrifying demands. God commanded Abraham to kill his son Isaac, and Abraham took every step to comply; obviously Abraham believed that the command of God superseded the law of his own country against homicide. There is no record that the legal authorities ever tried Abraham for attempted murder, but most would concede that this was a very special case. No law in the modern world condones killing professedly done by divine command.

In all probability, there will be more and more criticism of the annual State Department reports on international human freedom. Its subject matter is sensitive, and people have diverse and contradictory views on what international law should say about religious freedom. But the initial reports of the State Department display accommodation and balance. They strive to be nonjudgmental, but by their nature they quietly take positions on certain issues.

The report on Turkmenistan records a "crackdown on local Christian churches." In December 1999 the government began deporting foreigners suspected of missionary activities. Similarly, the report notes that the 1991 Ukraine law on freedom of conscience and religion provides for the separation of church and state but that some minorities and nontraditional religions are not receiving equal treatment.

The report on Algeria seems restrained and very cautious. The constitution of Algeria declares Islam to be the state religion but prohibits discrimination based on religious belief. The vast majority of citizens belong to the Sunni branch of Islam. No official data are available on the number of non-Muslim residents, but many non-Muslims fled Algeria during the eight-year conflict there between self-proclaimed radical Muslims and modern Muslims. Some 100,000 civilians and military personnel were killed in Algeria during the 1990s.

The study of Islam is required in Algeria's schools; no private primary or secondary schools are permitted to operate. Non-Islamic proselytizing is illegal, and the importation of non-Islamic literature for distribution is forbidden. The Shari'a-based family code prohibits Muslim women from marrying non-Muslims, although Muslim men can marry non-Muslim women.

The State Department's report on Algeria speaks for itself. Algeria is almost a theocracy, although it pretends to be tolerant of non-Islamic citizens. One has to ask how much Algeria would have to change if the basic principles of the United Nations Declaration on Religious Freedom were enforced. The 26.1 million people in Algeria must certainly feel the oppressive tactics of their government. The frank report of the U.S. Department of State describes the oppression of non-Muslims in Algeria in graphic, if subdued, tones. Will such reports be

helpful to the people of Algeria as the revelations about repression are refined and distributed around the world?

A similarly discouraging report on Bahrain was filed by
the State Department in 2000. That nation, from which about
40 percent of its population have emigrated, prohibits the presence of anti-Islamic writings. The Sunni Muslim minority en-
joys a favored status in government employment. Shi'a Muslims are openly denied positions in the defense or internal
security forces.

The State Department's 1999 and 2000 reports on religious freedom around the world constitute the first comprehensive catalog ever produced on this topic. Before they were
released, Kevin Boyle and Juliet Sheen's *Freedom of Religion
and Belief,* issued in 1997, was the most comprehensive collection of information about religious freedom around the world,
and it is still an excellent resource.

The State Department accounts of religious freedom in
India and China are, of course, central to any assessment of the
status of the free expression of religion in the world. Well over
2 billion people reside in these two nations. Neither Christianity nor Islam has ever had a significant presence in either country since the partition of India in 1947. Pakistan, with its predominantly Muslim population, withdrew from India rather
than live under non-Muslim laws.

What would the enforcement of religious freedom, now a
part or almost a part of customary international law, mean to
these traditionally Hindu and Buddhist countries? The changes
in both countries but especially in China would be rapid and
spectacular. Would they yield to spokespersons for Christianity and Islam? Their rigid opposition to missionaries gives
some idea of the stern resistance to outside forces that has always characterized these two giants, particularly China.

Will the content of the annual State Department reports have significant impact on the world's consciousness of religious freedom? The answer has to be yes, but all denial of religious freedom around the world is intertwined with history, politics, and even language. It seems that even if nations miraculously wanted to grant religious freedom, they would be hindered from doing so by all the intractable issues involved in ethnic backgrounds, historical entanglements, and resistance by political figures forced to choose between political survival and support of religious freedom.

The reporters of the state of religious rights in the world must openly face the fact that the Koran is the controlling factor in some forty Islamic states. Article XXII of the 1990 Cairo Declaration on Human Rights states that freedom is allowed if it "would not be contrary to the principles of the Shari'a." This compendium of Muslim law, put together more than a thousand years ago, has enormous implications for world law on human rights, as we shall see in Chapter 11.

With the enactment of the IRFA, the United States has, in essence, proclaimed to the world that it is a self-appointed defender of religious freedom in 190 nations. If "defender" is too strong a word, the United States has at least assumed the role of explainer and clarifier of the importance of religious freedom. If any other nation tried to do the same, its conduct would be criticized. But somehow the newly assumed role of the United States as the champion of religious freedom has not provoked overt hostility. The United States' aggressiveness in its new role, however, may deepen the antagonism of some Muslims, while other observers may think that the United States' initiative is naive, self-congratulatory, and even self-righteous.

What is clearly demonstrated by the United States' unilateral actions in support of religious freedom is that significant groups of religious persons have employed their political power to have the United States pronounce to the world its devotion to the free exercise of religion. However, the State Department's 1999 and 2000 reports have inadvertently revealed that the dimensions of religious freedom in the pantheon of internationally recognized human rights are not very clear at all.

Questions abound. Does the official designation of a national religion per se discriminate against the followers of other religions? How far can a nation go in promoting a religion on the grounds that the social and moral values of that religion are necessary for the well-being of the nation? Are there objective guidelines as to how much financial aid can be given to the religious bodies of a country? Are Islamic countries entitled to make reservations to treaties that declare that they will be bound by treaties only so far as their terms do not violate the principles of the Shari'a?

It is agreed that the norms expressed in the 1970 UN Declaration on Religious Freedom allow for a certain amount of diversity and pluralism. But at what point does it become clear that a government is too favorable to the majority religion or too unfavorable to religious minorities? These questions are hardly raised in the State Department reports. If commissions or tribunals were established with respect to religious freedom, those questions would come up and eventually be resolved. Defining the bounds of religious freedom is as troublesome as measuring the right to free speech, the right to privacy, or the right not to incriminate oneself. But the right to worship God and to follow his directives is more complex than any other right, because it assumes that persons of faith are required to act as their God and their consciences direct them to do, no matter how ill-advised their actions may seem to persons who do not share their religious faith.

The State Department's initial reports on religious freedom indicate how complex the topic will continue to be. Unfortunately, the reports have not received wide attention. They have not yet created an incentive for a worldwide independent nongovernmental agency to study the state of religious freedom. Observers of the State Department reports may have quietly concluded that no universal assessment of the state of religious freedom is really possible. Such a conclusion has some merit, although in the end any observer of human rights will have to agree that the freedom to practice one's religion is just as measurable as the rights to free speech, free press, and assembly.

But the complexity of the issue needs to be given full attention. In Afghanistan, for example, eight foreigners were jailed in 2001 on charges of preaching Christianity in efforts to convert Muslims. The Taliban, which then controlled at least 90 percent of the country, espoused a strict brand of Islam that considered any attempt to convert Muslims to be a crime. The Taliban raided the office of a German-based Christian agency called Vision for Asia and seized cassettes and literature that had been translated into local languages. The penalty for Afghans found guilty of proselytizing was death.

It seems easy to classify this as an extreme case attributable to fanaticism. But the presumably sincere conviction of the Muslims involved must receive a certain amount of deference. If these Muslims felt that they had a duty to protect their own people against being deprived of their God-given faith, we cannot simply discredit their position on the basis that the right to proselytize takes precedence over the right of the adherents of a faith to protect their fellow believers.

Could there ever be adequate international norms and judicial machinery to hear the contending sides of questions like this and issue rulings that would be binding even on regimes such as the Taliban? If such a tribunal had existed, could it have compelled the leaders of the Afghan government to yield to its decrees? That question reveals the enormous difficulties inherent in rendering international judgments contrary to the will of sovereign nations that adhere to particular religions. Even if such a judgment could be classified as binding under customary international law, the world and international law still seem reluctant to force a nation or a group of religious believers to act contrary to their conscience. A consensus on some basic issues in the area of religious freedom might develop at the global level—and it could happen soon— but the possibility of forming definitive, enforceable guidelines on religious freedom deriving from customary international law is remote.

Suppose the prohibition of abortion, except in very rare circumstances, were to be recognized as customary international law. This could happen if it were determined that Muslims, Hindus, Christians, and others around the world all converged in moral and spiritual agreement on the topic. The binding power of this norm, clearly required in this example by customary international law, would be strongly resisted by some Americans. These Americans would protest that U.S. law is set forth in *Roe v. Wade* and its progeny, and this law cannot be reversed by any contrary ruling based on customary international law or, for that matter, even by a ruling of *jus cogens,* a higher form of international law that decrees that some practices are so abhorrent that all nations must absolutely ban them.

Similarly, if international law recognized a guarantee of the right to proselytize, some Muslim leaders would claim that such a law was not binding on their countries. They would argue that, notwithstanding customary international law, the higher authority in their communities is the Koran or Shari'a, which clearly forbids attempts to convert Muslims.

An issue similar to proselytizing is blasphemy. In 2001 the Pakistani high court rejected the appeal of Ayub Masih, a Christian charged with blasphemy against Islam. Masih was arrested in 1996 for allegedly making derogatory remarks against the prophet Muhammad. Laws against blasphemy have generally not been enforced in recent years, but when, as in this case, a government does take such an action to protect the members of a religious group from weakening influences, the matter raises the question how international law should balance the rights of believers on opposing sides.

The U.S. Commission on International Religious Freedom is regularly asked to condemn violations of religious freedom. In August 2000 the commission nominated Burma, Iran, Iraq, Laos, North Korea, Saudi Arabia, Sudan, and Turkmenistan for designation by the State Department as "countries of particular concern." It also redesignated the now-deposed Taliban regime in Afghanistan as a "particularly severe violator of religious freedom."

The State Department's reports are a source of facts that were hitherto unavailable, but there are other sources, including the reports of the rapporteurs appointed by the United Nations Human Rights Commission and the UN Human Rights Committee. These documents have been issued for several years and have been deemed to be objective, neutral, and fair. I recall meeting with one UN rapporteur who visited the United States to investigate a few complaints and to give balance to his impressions of the comparative state of religious freedom in several countries.

One must conclude that the amount and quality of information on the state of religious freedom in the world has grown over the past several years. But the information still needs to be assessed in the light of some basic norms, some of which are still evolving.

The role of the United States, for better or for worse, may become more central and crucial than it is now. But the growing awareness of the uncertain state of religious freedom may lead to the emergence of other public and private reporting agencies that will focus on the multifaceted dilemmas that face everyone who wants to fashion a set of satisfactory principles that will bestow on religious freedom the status that it deserves under international law.

Ultimately, the United States' views have great influence on the UN's efforts to promote religious freedom. The world press writes regularly that the level of church attendance is higher in the United States than elsewhere. The vitality of religion-affiliated schools, hospitals, and social agencies in the United States is reported everywhere, and observers have noted the Bush administration's program to make public funds available to faith-based social welfare agencies. And of course everyone in the human rights community knows that the state of religious freedom in the world is reported and extensively commented on by the U.S. State Department's new agency on religious freedom.

Yet the United States is reluctant to extend religious freedom through instruments related to the United Nations, such as the 1981 Declaration on Religious Freedom. While the United States does denounce the repression of religion in nations such as China and Sudan, it does so unilaterally. The United States' reluctance or refusal to collaborate with the UN's machinery to supervise international human rights puts a damper on interest in strengthening international efforts to promote religious freedom. Although it is understandable that the United States is not eager to enter turbulent waters, the United States must recognize that it has the unique credibility to lead a discussion at the international level on the parameters of religious freedom and the corresponding rights of nonbelievers.

The formulators of U.S. public policy in 2002 spoke primarily of terrorism and the need for vigilance. This restricted outlook ignores many of the moral concepts that undergird international law. The idea of declaring war on terrorists goes against the spirit and the letter of the UN Charter, which said for the first time in history that no nation can declare war without the consent of other nations. The unilateral actions taken by the United States suggest that it considers itself above international conventions and believes it has a right to make war without regard to the opinion of the human family.

What the U.S. government rarely mentions is the fact that the terrorists who struck on September 11, 2001, acted, at least partially, as part of a jihad inspired by a religious concept. If the United States is to understand and effectively deal with this aggression, it has to try to comprehend the profound motivations of the men who sponsored the attacks and those who carried them out.

It is clear that the terrorists' attacks were motivated somewhat by religious concepts. The United States' ignorance of these ideas is a manifestation of its failure—and indeed the failure of the West—to see beyond the perimeters of nations that have been predominantly Christian for centuries. Many people throughout the world believe that Christianity and all religions have become marginal in the law and public morality of Western countries. The foreign policy of these nations, they claim, is dominated by notions of utilitarianism, pragmatism, and sheer short-term self-interest.

The United States is confronting terrorists who are acting out of a faith that is rooted in the Koran and from a detestation of Western nations—especially the United States. Some Muslims feel an active contempt for nations that act for their own self-aggrandizement, and they believe that the United States exemplifies this vice. For its part, the United States, despite its self-proclaimed devotion to religion, has not even tried to enter the minds of these extremists, perhaps because they represent only a tiny sector of the world's billion Muslims.

In *What Went Wrong? Western Impact and Middle Eastern Response* Bernard Lewis recounts the millennium of glory brought to the world by Islam and how the Muslim world lost virtually all of it. What remains is rage, self-pity, and a "downward spiral of hate and spite." Muslim nations have suffered conquest by colonial powers and wonder what they should do about their religion, which is rooted in the belief that all truth was revealed to their prophet. The resort to terrorism by a handful of adherents can be countered only if the United States tries to understand the religious roots of the men who authorized and carried out the September 11 attacks.

If a United Nations tribunal on religious freedom existed, its members would now be holding hearings and commissioning studies to help the world understand the source and meaning of the rage that prompted the savage attacks on the United States. As it is, religion surely has not been widely studied as a cause of some of the awful tragedies in recent years. Nevertheless, it is religion—or its absence—that is at the root of many of the repressions seen in the former USSR, in China, in the Balkans, and now in the attacks by Islamic terrorists.

International law has, in general, been silent on religion. The book *Religion and International Law,* edited by Mark Janis and Carolyn Evans, reports on this topic in detail. But it is clear that understanding the proper place of religion in society and affirming the need for religious freedom is central to the future of international society. Some framers of international law, including some in the United States, operate as if religion were a private matter that had little relevance to the formulation of a stable international society. Nothing could be further from the truth.

V

Religious Freedom and the
European Court of Human Rights

If one is looking for the prototype of a world court that resolves cases involving religious freedom, the first tribunal to evaluate is the European Court of Human Rights (ECHR). An excellent book on this topic, *Freedom of Religion under the European Convention on Human Rights,* by Carolyn Evans, offers reasons to see the approach followed by the ECHR as promising. It also, however, offers reasons to question the extent to which any judicial review can set boundary lines between the aspirations of religious persons and the demands of the state. Even laws guaranteeing religious freedom are strained in the cases of religious dissidents, conscientious objectors to military service, and persons who seek exemptions from legal restraints they deem to be contrary to their consciences. The ECHR has struggled in its efforts to support the right to religious freedom in these contexts.

But if the record of the ECHR is somewhat disappointing, it must also be recognized that no instant resolutions of the classic clashes between religion and government are feasible. In fact, the time may never come when the demands of government will be consistently required to yield to the lean-ings of individuals who are conscientiously opposed to a law of general application that unintentionally conflicts with their religious views. However, the whole thrust of the amazing de-velopment in international human rights law is that society and its legal institutions must now listen to and heed argu-ments based on conscience much more closely than in the past. Modern international law makes clear that domestic laws may be forced to yield to international standards of human rights, including the right to religious freedom.

The European Commission and Court of Human Rights, now merged into the ECHR, were established in 1953, after the horror of the Holocaust aroused Europeans' consciences to the plight of victims who had no forum of any kind in which to bring their complaints. So motivated, Europe did not wait for a worldwide tribunal to be established; it confessed its sorrow and pledged that judicial machinery would be established to allow every individual whose religious beliefs were violated to have an impartial tribunal hear his or her claim.

Before November 11, 1998, the European Commission and Court of Human Rights operated on complicated and du-plicative procedures. As a result, some claims based on reli-gious freedom were deemed not admissible on legal or proce-dural grounds. Ultimately, one of the reasons for the collapse of the commission into the court was the rising number of ap-plicants. In 1999, 8,356 applications were made to the court—a staggering increase over those of previous years.

An evaluation of the approach to religious freedom taken by that tribunal over the years is necessarily disappointing to observers who support a system that would allow generous ex-emptions for persons who cannot, in conscience, conform to state laws. The court is not unique in its shortcomings. Most courts in most nations, including the United States, are not especially generous in handling the complaints of persons who are conscientiously opposed to what the government considers important policies. Even when such claimants are successful, the success is often qualified. Although some citizens opposed to wartime military service may receive concessions as conscientious objectors, for example, their status and future are seldom equal to those of the individual who agrees to serve.

Moreover, the effort to get those concessions is usually lengthy and expensive. Few laws specify exemptions for religious dissidents. It is doubtful, for example, that any tax law in the world exempts taxpayers who in conscience oppose some objective of the law.

Even in Europe, with its comparatively expansive protections, there remains a certain hypocrisy in inserting provisions for dissenters on the basis of faith or belief into national or continental law but requiring those dissenters to travel to Strasbourg to litigate their claims. Yet the present European system is preferable to the situation before 1953: at least a tribunal is now available.

The cases brought before the ECHR are quite diverse. The plaintiffs include dissidents, gypsies, conscientious objectors, political prisoners, and similarly situated people among the continent's 400 million inhabitants. Even the legal backgrounds of the judges, although in some ways similar, reveal diversities of opinion on the nature of the law and the role of the judiciary.

Many of the ECHR's rulings may seem routine, but it must be remembered that they are being issued on a continent where minority groups have been persecuted for their religions since before the time of the Roman Empire. Heretics and nonbelievers were commonly subjected to torture and the most painful deaths that ingenuity could devise. The Crusades, the Inquisition, and the Holocaust are part of the collective memory of Europe. Also among Europeans' recollections is the syllabus of errors of 1864, when Pope Pius IX condemned the idea that the church should be separated from the state.

Notwithstanding this terrible history, the rulings of the ECHR have had great impact on the views that European nations hold toward religious rights. Their influence on the United Kingdom has been especially notable. Since Parliament's passage of the Human Rights Act of 1998, the United Kingdom has, in essence, agreed that in controverted issues related to civil rights and civil liberties, it will be bound by the rulings of the court in Strasbourg.

In many ways, Europe is breaking new ground with its law on religious freedom. Language on religious freedom in the European Convention on Human Rights is the forerunner of similar language in the United Nations documents on the freedom of religion.

Article 9 of the European Convention reads as follows:

1. Everyone has the right to freedom of thought, conscience and religion; this right includes freedom to change his religion or belief, and freedom, either alone or in community with others and in public or private, to manifest his religion or belief, in worship, teaching, practice and observance.
2. Freedom to manifest one's religion or belief shall be subject only to such limitations as are prescribed by law and are necessary in a democratic society in the interests of public safety, for the

> protection of public order, health or morals, or
> for the protection of the rights and freedoms of
> others.

The limitations on the rights to religious freedom contained in the European Convention include, it should be noted, those that "are necessary in a democratic society in the interests of public safety." Disappointingly, the phrase looks quite elastic, and what might be considered to be "usual" provisions on the rights of parents to educate their children in a way compatible with their own convictions proved to be so controversial that the acknowledgment of this freedom had to be postponed and placed in a separate protocol.

If some of the ECHR's approaches to religion seem to be overly deferential to the states, one must remember that the court was designed to adjudicate cases arising in countries with common cultures and, in general, deep respect for differences in religious background. As a result, the court resolves many challenges to alleged discrimination against religion by a doctrine known as the "margin of appreciation." This term indicates that the ECHR assumes at its discretion that the national lawmaking groups in Europe got it right when they decided issues of religious freedom. This policy is roughly equivalent to the presumption of constitutionality that the courts in the United States employ when they review laws. But this legal procedure in the United States does not seem to protect legislators as much as the "margin of appreciation" protects European lawmakers on legal questions involving religious freedom.

The 1978 decision of the ECHR in *Arrowsmith v. United Kingdom* illustrates the key question of how thorough or expansive the court should be in its rulings. Pat Arrowsmith, a committed pacifist, was found guilty of distributing leaflets to soldiers that urged them to refuse a tour of duty in Northern Ireland. Ms. Arrowsmith was not prosecuted when she was first discovered distributing the leaflets. When she and her colleagues then went to another army base and gave out their leaflets, the police asked them to desist, and all but Ms. Arrowsmith did so. She was subsequently arrested and prosecuted under a 1934 English law that prohibits any person from maliciously urging any member of the armed forces to leave his duty. Ms. Arrowsmith was found guilty by a jury and sentenced to eighteen months in prison. On appeal, her sentence was reduced to time served, but the conviction was sustained.

In a divided vote, the ECHR confirmed the conviction on the basis that Ms. Arrowsmith's pamphlet openly appealed not to pacifism but only to politics. A majority of the court pointed out that the pamphlet could have been distributed by persons who were opposed to the conflict in Northern Ireland not on religious grounds but for political reasons.

The narrow ground adopted by the majority was repudiated by Judge Klacker in his dissent. He opined that the distribution of the leaflets was an integral part of Ms. Arrowsmith's belief and therefore should be protected under Article 9 of the covenant. The court, he reasoned, should look at the entire scene and allow the challenged conduct if the person involved acted out of convictions that were an integral part of her life philosophy. He theorized that the narrow view taken by the majority had the potential to undermine the right of religious freedom.

The differing views expressed in *Arrowsmith* permeate the cases brought before the ECHR in respect to issues related to religious freedom. Generally the narrow, confining approach of the majority in *Arrowsmith* prevails. The consistent view is that the challenged action cannot be invalidated unless it resulted from an action directly required or compelled by one's religious faith or belief.

The test employed by the majority in *Arrowsmith* seems to be whether the applicant acted in a way that is *required* by his or her religion. But this test leads to all sorts of subjectivity and ambiguity, as is evident in the case law. In *Kahn v. United Kingdom* (1986), the European Commission upheld the conviction of a man who went through an Islamic marriage ceremony with a fourteen-year-old girl, contrary to the wishes of her parents. In Islamic law, the age at which a girl can marry without her parents' consent is twelve, whereas in British law it is eighteen. The commission upheld the sentence of nine months, finding that Mr. Kahn's religion allowed him to marry an underaged girl, but it did not require him to do so. It is arguable that the decision diminished, if not defied, the claim of religious freedom.

In *X v. Austria* (1981), the ECHR upheld the decision of the Austrian government to stop a "Moonie sect" from establishing a legal association on the basis that such an association was not required for the practice of their beliefs.

In *X v. United Kingdom* (1974), the ECHR ruled that Britain was not required to allow a Buddhist prisoner to send articles to a Buddhist magazine, because the prisoner was unable to prove that transmitting the letters was necessary to the practice of his religion.

Malcolm Evans has summarized the record of the ECHR on religious freedom in his book *Religious Liberty and International Law in Europe*. Evans clearly states that fidelity to a religion need not be without cost, and he demonstrates the burden and even the penalties that are sometimes placed on religions—especially those that go against the mainstream.

In struggling to define the scope of religious freedom, the ECHR and the whole world look to the several decisions of the

U.S. Supreme Court that interpret the right to religious freedom guaranteed by the First Amendment to the U.S. Constitution. Until recently the Court's record was praiseworthy. Reversing a prior ruling, for example, the Court forbade a school to expel the children of Jehovah's Witnesses who could not, in conscience, salute the flag. The Supreme Court also gave relief to Amish children whose parents insisted that they could not, in good conscience, allow their children to attend school beyond the eighth grade.

That generosity to religious dissidents in the United States seems to have ended in 1990 with *Smith v. Oregon.* In a 5–4 decision, the Supreme Court reversed a ruling of the Supreme Court of Oregon to hold that persons of Indian ancestry would not be exempted from a law banning the use of peyote, even for sacramental purposes. Subsequently, the Congress in essence tried to reverse this decision by enacting the Religious Freedom Restoration Act, but that law also was struck down by the Supreme Court as an interference by the Congress in the Court's power to define and enforce the First Amendment. The protection extended to religious freedom by both the ECHR and the U.S. Supreme Court now seem unclear, uncertain, and unpredictable.

Obviously a war of conflicting ideas is going on. One must recognize that the ECHR was established so that members of minority religions in Europe would never be left without resources if a nation set out to destroy them, as Germany did the Jews. But the European Convention on Human Rights does not merely forbid the destruction of a religious group; it also gives every person of faith and every faith-based body the right to go to an all-European tribunal to get relief. The idea is noble.

Opinions on the ECHR's effectiveness differ. Members of minority religions are generally not enthusiastic about the way they have been treated by the judges in Strasbourg. Observers more supportive of Strasbourg's idiosyncratic religious rulings warn that society cannot make too many concessions to groups with unpopular positions.

The ECHR reveals the best and the worst in the handling of claims against governments on the grounds of discrimination based on faith or belief. The court has offered a sympathetic ear to claims grounded on allegations of the infringement of religious liberty, but it has also reflected the views of a continent that has been Christian for centuries. The judges on the ECHR would deny that they unconsciously reflect the values of their background. But their opinions seem to be unsympathetic to Europe's non-Christians. The court's precedents are unlikely to encourage Muslims and other non-Christians—an ever-growing portion of Europe's population—to hope for rulings supporting a new pluralism based on a more expansive right to the free exercise of religion.

In the final analysis, religious freedom will continue to be denied until political leaders fully grasp the effects of this denial. It demeans people of faith. It can even reduce religious citizens in their own eyes, because they can be forbidden to do things they embrace as the very heart of their persona. Restrictions on the religious freedoms of non-Christians in Europe will also deepen their feelings of being strangers in a strange land. It may be too strong to associate infringements on religious freedoms with torture; but rulings against a right to religious dress or a right for Muslims to pray at noon, for example, will tell Muslims and other religious minorities that their religions are less important than the convenience of the public.

The ECHR has not addressed some potentially thorny issues. One question it has not really taken up is Germany's requirement that all taxpayers reveal their church or religion—usually Catholic or Lutheran—and have a significant part of their taxes withheld to support the church they designate. Tax-payers can theoretically opt out of a church and cease to pay the ecclesiastical levy, but most citizens do not take that step. Will the ECHR eventually decree that Germany cannot continue this practice?

One of the major reasons for the creation of the ECHR was the wish to establish a legal framework that would prevent religious groups from being persecuted as the Jews were under Hitler. It was and remains a noble mission. But it is not entirely clear that the ECHR would be able to accomplish that mission if European leaders began to repeat the mistakes of the Third Reich.

VI

Vatican II Vigorously
Defends Religious Freedom

Efforts to develop the right to religious freedom often center on attempts to influence the actions of nations and political leaders. Politically elected or appointed authorities are frequently urged to recognize international law and maximize the freedom of every religious believer or group in their territories. The leaders of churches, synagogues, and mosques, however, are seldom reminded of the parameters of international law. This is not an oversight; one of the basic assumptions in international law is that the actions of private parties are not under its jurisdiction. In this paradigm, only nations, never individuals, can claim violations of international law or be held responsible for such violations.

But in recent years this traditional view has given way to the opinion that individuals possess some rights and even some obligations under international law. For example, an optional protocol attached to several international covenants on human rights allows individual citizens to bring claims directly to international entities when they believe that their own nations have denied their rights under international law.

Purely religious bodies, however, have not yet been recognized as having standing in international law. Religious entities have been assumed to be beyond the control of the organizations that create laws binding on nations. Even where international law does deal with religion, it does so in general terms, without reference to any specific religion, much less to the conduct of any particular church, synagogue, or mosque. As a result, the religious bodies of the world are to a large extent free to be as zealous or aggressive as they feel their creed allows or compels, without regard for the equal treatment of other religions. In fact, religious bodies are usually deemed to be subject to less regulation under secular law, national or international, than most other private bodies. Religious groups are, in other words, unique in the human family.

Religious groups through the centuries have sometimes taken advantage of their unique status and have sometimes abused it. At least that is the consensus today, especially in view of the revolutionary position taken in 1965 by the Second Vatican Council. An appreciation of its statements requires a retelling of some history.

From their beginnings, both Judaism and Christianity have more or less assumed that they were destined to create a culture and form a society. The formation of a theocracy seemed to be the accepted path to follow.

The Jewish Bible assumes and asserts that God's people are to live together in order to ward off enemies and to create a civilization of their own. The evolution of Judaism is unique, because one of its fundamental missions was to await the coming of the Messiah. In view of this divine mission, the idea that the Jewish people should hold themselves separate seems perfectly reasonable. The Romans' destruction of the temple of Solomon in 70 AD and the dispersal of the Jewish people seemed to obliterate the Jews' prophetic mission to create a society under the immediate direction of the God of Abraham, Isaac, and Jacob. Of all the extant religious groups in the world, the Jewish people now probably have the least aspiration for theocracy.

In 315 AD the Christians deliberately assumed the ancient Hebrew belief that the Church of God was destined to call all the peoples of the world together and form a society that would unite and serve God and all his people. That Christian goal remained active for centuries and has never been completely set aside. It still seems plausible to some Christians that Christianity, being divinely established, may bring all things spiritual and secular under its dominion. The Bible seems to give several justifications for this ambition.

In retrospect, the Catholic hegemony of Europe for a thousand years raises countless questions about the propriety of this arrangement. From today's perspective, the Crusades, the Inquisition, and dozens of other actions of "Christendom" are embarrassing. The overall impression one gets of that age is of a time when the Church dominated all aspects of life, secular and political as well as religious. Although this is possibly an incomplete or unfair way of looking at a millennium of history, it does seem now that the linking of religion and government for all those centuries was not beneficial to either.

The present-day disdain for anything approaching a theocracy is deep and presumably irreversible. There is a profound and powerful feeling that religion should not be intermingled with the government and that the government should not depend on religion. That feeling—probably more deeply held in the United States than elsewhere—is, if one looks at most cultures, naive and unrealistic. Essentially every culture depends on some preexisting set of moral or religious beliefs or customs. The Hindu religion was so deep-seated in the culture of India that it survived and to some extent countered the British occupation of that nation. Buddhism has always been the soul of China in hard-to-define ways, notwithstanding the anti-religious attitudes of its current Communist government. The 200 million indigenous people of the world continue to live by ancient codes that they believe have divine or transcendental qualities. The Muslim nations possibly offer the most dramatic example of the inseparability of moral or religious codes and governments: it is simply assumed in many, if not most, Islamic countries that the truths of the religion of the prophet Muhammad and the Muslim code of law, the Shari'a, form the basis of the civil law and are a prerequisite to any moral commitment that a Muslim nation gives to the commands of international law.

With all of that history, what can the United Nations do to harmonize these distinct and deeply held traditional religious values with a world community seeking to adapt its people to the unbelievable changes of the new millennium? The covenants issued by the United Nations on human, political, and economic rights have changed the way the entire world relates to these concepts. Indeed, the paradigm shifts that have attended the codification of internationally recognized human rights are so pervasive and omnipresent that they defy description.

But the international community has not yet grappled with the place of religion in modern society. The United Nations Declaration on Religious Freedom, issued in 1981, has stimulated discussions, but it is not specific enough to bring about major changes. At the moment, the international law of religious freedom is quiescent, although few believe that it can remain inactive for long. Forces that affect the place of religion in international law will shortly be calling out for discussion and resolution at the highest levels.

Amidst all this global political uncertainty about the place of religion at the national and international levels, the Catholic Church engaged in a worldwide debate on the matter and for the first time endorsed a principle of church-state separation. The Catholic Church's Declaration on Religious Freedom, after years of debate within religious circles, was adopted on December 7, 1965, at the Second Vatican Council.

I followed that debate for ten years before Vatican II. Many eminent theologians of that time approved the centuries-old adage that "error has no rights" and that governments therefore have an obligation to prefer, even exalt, the "true faith." The confessional state was put forward as the ideal. I must say that the arguments for the traditional position were strong, supported by papal decrees and appealing to believers who felt obliged to call upon the good offices of government to support the "true religion."

John Courtney Murray, S.J., the theologian who did more than anyone else to bring about the Declaration on Religious Freedom, had been prohibited from writing about church-state relations by the Holy See. He was invited to the council as a peritus, however, and he helped to formulate a decree that altered forever the academic, political, and legal issues involved in separating the things that belong to Caesar and the things that belong to God. Discussing the Declaration on Religious Freedom in his book *The Decrees of Vatican II*, Father Murray recalls that the Second Vatican Council conducted "the greatest argument on religious freedom in all history." After the council released its Declaration on Religious Freedom, Murray rejoiced that a new era in history had arrived; the Church no longer dealt with the world in terms of a double standard—

"freedom for the church when Catholics are in a minority, and privilege for the church and intolerance for others when Catholics are in a majority." The Declaration on Religious Freedom has generated a whole library of books of commentary. One noteworthy example is *John Paul II and the Legacy of Dignitatis Humanae,* by the Portuguese Jesuit Hermino Rico.

The final Declaration on Religious Freedom is, in fact, the sixth version of a document that proved to be the most difficult and controversial of any undertaken by the council fathers from 1962 to 1965. The powerful and cogent final document opens by reaffirming the long-held position of the Catholic Church in these words:

> The religious acts whereby men, in private and in public, and out of a sense of personal conviction, direct their lives to God transcend by their very nature the order of terrestrial and temporal affairs. Government, therefore, ought indeed to take account of the religious life of the people and show it favor since the function of government is to make provision for the common welfare. However, it would clearly transgress the limits set to its power were it to presume to direct or inhibit acts that are religious.

This paragraph sets the tone for the entire document: government has some duty to "show favor" to religion, but may not "presume to direct or inhibit acts that are religious."

The document points out that church and other religious groups both have a right to give witness to faith, but "in spreading religious faith and introducing religious practices, everyone ought at all times to refrain from any manner of action which might seem to carry a hint of coercion or of a kind of persuasion that would be dishonorable or unworthy." This statement—probably the heart of the declaration—could hardly be more forceful. No "hint of coercion" may be used in spreading religious faith.

At the same time, the document makes clear that religion has a crucial role in society. It "comes within the meaning of religious freedom that religious bodies should not be prohibited from freely undertaking to show the special value of their doctrine in what concerns the organization of society and the inspiration of the whole of human activity." The protection of religious freedom is, moreover, one of the "essential duties of government."

The council fathers recognized that not every nation is likely to abolish an arrangement whereby some preference is given to one religion or for the establishment of one church. But the admonition to governments is strong: "A wrong is done when government imposes upon its people, by force or fear or other means, the professional repudiation of any religion, or when it hinders men from joining or leaving a religious body."

The Vatican declaration continues by affirming the need for international protection of human rights: "All the more is it a violation of the will of God and of the sacred rights of the person and the family of nations when force is brought to bear in any way in order to destroy or repress religion either in the whole of mankind or in a particular country or in a specific community."

These Vatican decrees on religious freedom pronounced in 1965 were issued sixteen years before the United Nations Declaration on Religious Freedom, but the Vatican document firmly supports international protection for religious freedom. Its words are powerful:

> Religious freedom has already been declared to be a
> civil right in most constitutions, and it is solemnly
> recognized in international documents. A further
> fact is that forms of government still exist under
> which, even though freedom of religious worship
> receives constitutional recognition, the powers of
> government are engaged in the effort to deter citi-
> zens from the profession of religion and to make life
> difficult and dangerous for religious communities.

The council concludes its declaration with another affirmation of the need of global protection for religious freedom: "It is necessary that religious freedom be everywhere provided with an effective constitutional guarantee, and that respect be shown for the high duty and right of man freely to lead his religious life in society."

Only a handful of the council fathers voted against the statement on religious freedom. One of its most enthusiastic supporters was Archbishop Karol Wojtyla, later Pope John Paul II. Many papal statements made during the pontificate of John Paul II rely on the endorsement of religious freedom in the declarations of the Second Vatican Council. Vatican II obviously had an enormous impact on the declaration on religious freedom finally adopted by the UN General Assembly in 1981.

Few religious groups dissent from the work of Vatican II and the contents of the Declaration on Religious Freedom. The Catholic Church was praised for its advancement, even though the right to religious freedom accepted by the Church had been acknowledged by European society more than a century earlier. The Holy See's renunciation of rights its predecessors had long claimed transformed the image of the Church in important ways. Nor is the support from other religious bodies faint praise. Almost all religious groups are also uniformly in favor of the human rights endorsed by the United Nations. A fact-filled volume on this topic can be found in *Faith in Human Rights*, by Robert Traer.

The Vatican decree relies heavily on the concept that the right of religious freedom derives directly from the inherent dignity of every person. The document leaves no ambiguity on the foundation of the right. Other religious and secular proclamations on the right to worship or to be free from discrimination are also based on the argument that every person is entitled to respect for the basic reason that each person is unique and has a conscience.

The historic document on religious freedom issued by the Second Vatican Council makes it clear that the Church has taken a historic step away from several attitudes that it had held for centuries. Some of the new attitudes are still surprising to some Catholics. Of course, the council's declaration signaled an official shift in doctrine, albeit one long considered: indeed, several Vatican II documents echo views expressed by Church leaders during the development of the international human rights movement twenty years earlier. However, only the subsequent use of the concepts stated by the council as being inherent in the Church led to practices consistent with an enlarged concept of the equality of all persons.

The products of Vatican II leave many observers with a sense of enlightenment, hope, and inspiration. The council's work can be seen as the story of an ancient and venerable church meeting the modern world and reiterating and re-directing the rights newly recognized in that new universe. However, the Catholic Church is behind other religious groups. At the first assembly of the World Council of Churches (WCC) in Amsterdam in 1948, the Protestants and some groups of Orthodox Christians affirmed the need for "an international bill of rights." The declaration of the WCC asked for "adequate safeguards for freedom of religion and conscience." The Amsterdam declaration made it clear that Christians "do not ask for any privilege to be granted to Christians that is denied to others." The statement of the WCC remains a landmark in the evolution of religious freedom, as it was probably the first major statement on religious freedom that did not come from a historically disenfranchised and persecuted religious minority.

However, fundamental questions about the scope of religious freedom persist; for example, do the Vatican's vindication of religious freedom and the 1981 UN declaration share any common ground on the existence of a right for missionaries to enter a nation with the intent of preaching the Gospel? The Catholic Church and many missionary-minded Protestant and evangelical groups are intensely interested in the question. One would hope that missionaries in the future would be much more aware of the sensitivities of those whom they seek to influence, but the desire to evangelize or catechize is basic to the religious freedom of millions of people.

Parallel to this question is the issue of whether non-Christians have any right to privacy from missionaries who are "invading" their country. Do non-Catholic missionaries have a right to contact the native Catholics in Latin America, for example, or does the Church have the right to keep out religious workers who seek to change the religion of persons with whom they speak? Some may feel that international law has little to offer in this sticky situation, but there are rights on both sides, and an international tribunal might well offer assistance and reconciliation by adjudicating the competing positions.

Is it feasible to establish an international judicial body to hear the claims of persons who feel that their government is discriminating against their religion? The European Court of Human Rights in Strasbourg has been hearing cases of this kind; we have seen that the results are not always satisfactory. But in the 140 member states of the United Nations that are outside of Europe, many persons and groups feel that their governments are denying them freedom of religion. Unless the case can be framed as a violation of freedom of the press or something comparable, there is currently no forum in which a complaint can be brought. If an international tribunal were created to hear religious claims, persons who are denied the right to religious freedom in such places as China, India, and Muslim countries could have recourse to its protections.

Some observers will wonder whether a judgment favorable to a claimant would be worthwhile. After all, the existing government might not enforce it, or it might receive little publicity and thereby only harm the situation of the aggrieved party. But at least a voice of protest would have been heard and a complaint processed. One important moral justification for creating human rights tribunals is simply that they might prevent any recurrence of the situation in which Europe's Jews had no place to go to complain.

There is a remarkable convergence of opinion and action in the Vatican's and the UN's declarations on human rights, and few people oppose the principles expressed in them. How can legal and judicial machinery hope to do justice to a right that by common consent is sacred, precious, and esteemed by nearly everyone in the human family?

Is the United States silent on the issue of religious freedom around the world because its domestic situation in respect to religion is relatively good? Actually, the state of religious freedom in the United States does make it hard for human rights organizations to foster moral indignation in the population over abuses elsewhere. Things are not perfect in the United States, but outright intolerance and discrimination are not serious problems. It seems that the only U.S. groups vehemently protesting the denial of religious freedom are a unit of Freedom House and the Commission on Religious Freedom related to the U.S. State Department.

Nongovernmental organizations (NGOs) in the United States have been active on issues related to the persecution of Soviet Jews, the elimination of apartheid in South Africa, the global ban of land mines, the repression in Burma, and comparable topics. The entire world has witnessed the miracles that moral indignation have produced in these areas. Perhaps, however, most Americans somehow cannot really relate to discrimination against persons who are seeking only to exercise their religious rights. When Americans look abroad, they usually associate antireligious activities with ethnic, political, or economic difficulties rather than see them as human rights issues.

Would a new NGO devoted exclusively to religious freedom dramatize the cases of suppression or persecution of religion around the world? Amnesty International, established in 1963, was the first NGO to focus international attention on "prisoners of conscience" and comparable outrages. Aside from Freedom House, no prominent NGO is concentrating on violations of religious freedom. Of course, this issue overlaps with others, as the denial of the free exercise of religion often in-

volves international political and ethnic factors. Still, the anger
and activism that NGOs arouse for refugees, victims of ethnic
violence, and children maimed by land mines could be awak-
ened for those who are made to suffer for their religious convictions. But it is difficult to maintain such a level of public
support. The outrages to the Falun Gong in China made head-
lines, for example, but no well-informed and persistent public
campaign in support of this religious group is visible.

Some people sense that the press is less devoted to freedom of religion than to other humanitarian causes. Some have
claimed that the activities of religious groups are not adequately covered in the press. It has also been alleged that journalists, as a group, are generally less likely to attend religious
services than other professionals. While every bit of hard information on this topic is worthy of consideration, the reality
is that discrimination, overt or covert, against religion is more
difficult to uncover and report than many other abuses of
human rights.

Nevertheless, to some extent religion is off the radar
screen of a society that has silently agreed that the world of religion is nongovernmental and private, and therefore not appropriate for news coverage. No one takes the credit or the
blame for that state of things, but there is some kind of consensus that the world of religion is a no-man's-land for the
media. Those secular forces that, out of a concern for society,
isolate and exclude religion from their attention do perennial
harm to religion, but the whole issue is filled with dilemmas
and paradoxes.

In a sense, the Catholic Church in Vatican II recognized
the forces of secularism and gave up its seat at the table on
governmental affairs. It conceded the privatization of religion,
settling for assurances of tolerance and nondiscrimination

from government forces, and this is now the stance of every religious group in Western culture. This relationship will prevent some cases of open persecution, because religious bodies are no longer the rivals of the government. A truce has been reached, with religions disarmed—and, some would say, made to some extent irrelevant. Others, including many devout Christians who welcome the new status and role of religious organizations, go so far as to claim that the Church made a monumental mistake when it accepted the patronage of Constantine in the year 315.

In any event, the thrust of international law in this area should be to extend the guarantees of the Universal Declaration of Human Rights and the covenants on political rights to religion in all its forms. Religious citizens who are being openly oppressed in nations such as China and Sudan have a right to the firm support of the family of nations. Every member state of the United Nations, including Switzerland since 2001, has pledged in Articles 55 and 56 of the UN Charter to defend human rights. It is clear, however, that religious freedom is not receiving the attention that the members of the United Nations have pledged. The way to change that situation is less clear, but the Declaration on Religious Freedom made by the Second Vatican Council, along with the United Nations Declaration on Religion, offers the moral framework for a new and vigorous plan for the protection of the free exercise of religion.

The Declaration on Religious Freedom issued by the Second Vatican Council had a profound effect on Catholic thinking everywhere in the world. The traditionalists who had held that "error has no rights" seem to have almost disappeared since Vatican II. On the other hand, those who supported the Church's new thesis and tone on religious freedom quietly conceded that the Church had merely agreed to the ideas of religious freedom that had been accepted in Europe since at least 1800.

Even if the decree was slow in coming, the Church's statement repudiating the use of any kind of coercion to advance the faith was a cause for rethinking and rejoicing by Catholics. The acceptance of everyone's individual freedom to religious choice made sense by every theological norm used throughout the ages of faith. It is elementary in Catholic teaching that faith is a gift given gratuitously by God to those whom God chooses. No human effort can merit faith or expedite its coming. Such a concept was rejected when the Catholic Church repudiated every form of Pelagianism.

But Catholics, and possibly all believers, seem tribalistically to show rivalry and antagonism toward groups with other beliefs—feelings that can quickly grow into astonishingly bitter hostility. Such outbreaks of rancor have decreased remarkably since Vatican II, but one worries that this development might not be altogether favorable if it connotes indifference to the truth or falsity of religious claims that have distinguished Catholics and Protestants since the Reformation.

The decrees of Vatican II on religious freedom cut in many ways. The Catholic Church pledged not to place disabilities on other Christians or non-Christians who proselytize in Catholic nations. It asserted that no country should impose barriers to the existence and growth of non-Catholic religious groups.

More important, the *Dignitatis humanae* (its title is taken from the first two words of the Vatican II document on religious freedom) renounced the traditional teaching that governments have the right and sometimes the duty to protect "the true faith." Indeed, it now seems incredible that the Catholic Church held that position for such a long time. But the Second Vatican Council did not surrender to the doctrine that the government has no duty to religion except to tolerate it. Vatican II insisted in several ways that all governments need a moral and spiritual basis for their existence and for their laws. Some governments, including those in the Islamic world, can quote the document on religious freedom to endorse their voice on certain moral or religious values.

When the United Nations and the global community begin the task of clarifying and improving the United Nations 1981 Declaration on Religious Freedom, the *Dignitatis humanae* will be an essential part of the process. Theologians, jurists, and human rights activists can profitably study the history, the origins, and the dimensions of religious freedom as proclaimed by Vatican II. Furthermore, one of the dreams of the global international human rights movement is to apply the basic principles of equality and human dignity to religious wars and struggles. The declaration made by the Second Vatican Council will be an essential text and could even serve as the cornerstone of future efforts to achieve that goal.

After one has explored the full ramifications of the Vatican statement on religious freedom, the question has to be asked whether the full exercise of religious freedom would be available worldwide if the family of nations accepted and lived by that document. Although some lawyers and jurists would no doubt like to be able to answer in the affirmative, the truth may be that faith in the divine is not always subject to control and direction by human laws. Almost by its nature, faith in something supernatural cannot be controlled as if it were just another initiative or aspiration of human beings. Faith is not explainable, predictable, or controllable. It is above reason, and therefore is not understandable by the logic humankind employs to seek understanding of all things human. Nor is Christian faith always attainable, even by those who desire it and seek to make themselves worthy of it. Faith, as the Gospels and Catholic tradition from time immemorial have taught, comes only to those whom God has chosen for reasons that are as mysterious as the existence and essence of God himself.

VII

The Rights of Dissenters

Throughout history, the status granted to persons who do not have or do not profess religious faith has seldom been very favorable. The presence of believers has always been intensive and extensive, and persons who do not share the beliefs of the majority have frequently been persecuted. Romans faithful to their pantheon were intolerant of Christians; Catholics and Protestants, when they have been in charge of societies, have nearly always been intolerant of persons who disagreed with them.

The instinct of both governments and religious organizations to make themselves the exclusive force in society is equally prevalent in the Islamic world. Indeed, a unitary structure for society dominates the scene in Muslim countries. There the mosque and the government essentially form one unit. In nations where Hindus or Buddhists are the majority, the very concept of separation of government from religion is alien. Hence nonbelievers are often identified as individuals who are at odds, or even at war, with their fatherland.

Consequently, the newly recognized human rights of persons who do not adhere to the religious orthodoxy of their country represents a phenomenon very new in human history. Acknowledging such a right goes against all the instincts of those governments that desire a monopoly of power. The right to dissent also goes against the traditions of most churches, which by doctrine commonly think they should dominate the scene.

The idea of groups of nonbelievers or dissidents having rights that must be recognized by law is an unfamiliar concept. These are not groups of outspoken atheists or aggressive agnostics; the citizens claiming membership in these groups are usually quiet bystanders who have never held or have lost faith in the prevailing religious ethos. These citizens often feel secret resentment at the pressure that their societies place on them to ignore, or at least be silent about, their misgivings and doubts.

In the United States, public opinion polls indicate that some 80 percent or more of the population believe in God. At the same time, some 100 million people—or about one-third of the total U.S. population—have no formal affiliation with any religious body. In Europe, by contrast, polls reveal large numbers of citizens without religious faith and a remarkably high number who never go to church.

In the Muslim world, the figures for persons who adhere to Islam are very high. However, a creeping secularism in some Islamic countries may reveal the pressure of millions of people who do not, in fact, believe in the message of the prophet Muhammad.

One should therefore not lose sight of the millions of individuals who do not really believe in Christianity or Islam, though they feign acceptance. The traditionalists and the faithful, in evaluating the status of international human rights, often do not want to allow new standards of world morality to weaken bonds that law and public opinion have fashioned to buttress the status of traditional religions. The pressure that these well-organized religions place on persons who express various forms of dissent is subtle but strong.

When called upon to justify their reluctance to accept the developing rights of nonbelievers, the religious-minded may assert the need for faith and religion as the foundation stones of a good society. Although there is some obvious truth in this position, it tends to short-change nonbelievers by insinuating that they are a subversive force that undermines public morality. For many believers, this is a self-evident truth. For them the fate of the republic depends on God-fearing citizens whose morality is created, or at least reinforced, by a conviction that an all-just God rewards the good and punishes the wicked.

There is a certain logic to this approach to the good society. However, it is not consistent with the international law of human rights, which separates the power of Caesar from the mission of God. Modern-day human rights law does not exalt secularism, but it does insist that believers may not turn persons without faith into second-class citizens or worse. In other words, the United Nations documents on human rights are in agreement with the statements issued by the Second Vatican Council that persons without religious faith may not, directly or indirectly, be placed in a class or position that is beneath that of believers.

The contemporary tensions between governments and churches are nothing new in human history, but now organized religions have a warning from international law as well as from their own highest councils that they should not depend on governments to reinforce their structure and penalize those who have fallen away. Some few Christian bodies have followed this counsel for centuries. The Anabaptists and their progeny, for example, afraid that involvement with the government would diminish and even corrupt them, have always maintained a rigid separation between state and religion. Roger Williams boldly demonstrated that policy when he left Massachusetts and founded the state of Rhode Island on the basis of a radical separation of the church from the government.

The protection of the rights of believers, so carefully safeguarded in the United Nations statements on religious freedom, can be partially attributed to the fact that the authors of the United Nations Charter were, in general, people of faith. One cannot identify many open nonbelievers who were at the table when the modern world's human rights documents were hammered out. Even if some were there, they may well have been influenced by the hard-to-refute argument that persons who believe in religion are better citizens.

Moreover, those international covenants were authored by statesmen from the West. These drafters were familiar with the vague deism that is reflected in a few references to a divine being in the United Nations Charter and the Universal Declaration of Human Rights. They recognized the incompleteness of that approach and composed the UN Declaration on Religious Freedom eventually agreed to by the General Assembly in 1981.

There were no militant atheists or agnostics at the table when the United Nations was putting together the historic documents that have transformed the world forever. Even if nonbelievers had been there, they might well have accepted the guarantees of religious freedom that are contained in almost every UN document on human rights. In other words, nonbelievers do not necessarily want to curb the rights of those who believe. They desire only that believers be given no privileges that in essence turn nonbelievers into less than equal partners in decisions that formulate the public morality of their society.

Can there then be a bill of rights for nonbelievers? The authors of the United Nations Declaration on Religious Freedom would, in all probability, claim that their documents treat believers and nonbelievers with objectivity and impartiality. That may be so, but some nonbelievers would argue that the pro-religion traditions of the West and the orientation of the years after World War II contributed to an atmosphere that prompted some basic decisions to favor religion. Once again, however, nonbelievers might not have protested too vigorously, because in the entirely new universe that the West was entering after World War II, everyone felt that all kinds of moral guidance were needed.

In view of the world's adoption of many safeguards for the protection of the religious freedom of everyone, are there nonbelievers who feel that they have been singularly or collectively placed into a second class? If they feel that way, they have not been active or aggressive in announcing such a position. But silence does not necessarily mean that the nonbelievers of the world feel included or that they don't believe that United Nations documents confer a somehow privileged status on religion.

But when we assess the reaction of nonbelievers to the status given to religion by the United Nations documents, it is wise to recall the secret resentment over the semi-established state of religion in many European countries. Periodic outbursts against religion in the past four centuries in Europe reveal the barely concealed disdain for the Catholic Church held by the millions of Europeans who either do not follow Catholicism or do not believe in any organized religion.

Some will ask whether such sensitivity to the perspectives of nonbelievers is appropriate. In response, it is crucial to remind the whole world that the United Nations intended to grant no preference to any religion and that for the first time in the history of civilization a benevolent neutrality has been decreed for all religions. This decree cannot be expected to protect the place or the status of all nonbelievers, but each nonbeliever has a right not to feel inferior to, subordinated by, or excluded from his or her own society.

In her rulings on church-state issues, U.S. Supreme Court Justice Sandra Day O'Connor has wondered and worried whether the presence of religion—especially in the classroom—might leave the members of minority religions or nonreligious persons feeling diminished within their own society. The prevention of such statuses, however subtle, is one of the purposes of the guarantee of religious freedom contained in the First Amendment of the U.S. Constitution. It is also one of the objectives of the authors of the United Nations Declaration on Religious Freedom. Of course, some observers may wonder whether the exquisite neutrality called for in these important documents can be realized over the full range of settings to which they must be applied.

U.S. courts have always taken a friendly and favorable attitude toward all forms of organized religion. Although it is true that the Mormons were restricted in their practice of polygamy, massive tax exemptions for churches and privileges for the Amish, Jehovah's Witnesses, and others have passed muster in the U.S. Supreme Court. In the 1970 *Walz* decision, the Supreme Court sustained tax exemptions for religious groups. In reaching its conclusion, the Court relied on precedent going back to England, recognized that the idea enjoyed widespread acceptance, and noted that similar tax exemptions went to nonreligious groups. The issue has never been relitigated. In June 2002 the Supreme Court examined whether parents have the right to control the orientation of the education of their children and lent limited approval to the idea in a

5–4 decision favorable to the creation of some form of vouchers for private schools.

Nonbelievers have not harshly criticized the record of the U.S. Supreme Court, but one could argue that the Supreme Court has generally favored religions of all kinds. If the Court began to look to the Universal Declaration on Religious Freedom, would it be more favorable to persons with religious faith than to those without faith? Whether the declaration contains such a bias is an unanswerable and troublesome question involved in the struggle to give true equality to persons who do not have religious faith.

The difficulty of the quest is compounded by the pervasive unpopularity of persons who speak out strongly against organized religion. Because of this near-universal disdain, there are no doubt millions of nonbelievers who remain silent although they feel deeply that society and the law have conferred on religious entities privileges they have not granted to nonbelievers. Even when vocal, the critics of organized religion often find that they do not have a voice in the mainstream press. Nevertheless, such nonbelievers can be certain that the United Nations documents on religious freedom were designed to give them equality with those who adhere to organized religion.

Do persons hostile to religion feel that they have a place and a voice equal to those of churches or synagogues? If they do not, they will oppose strengthening the United Nations Declaration on Religious Freedom into a covenant that could eventually attain the status of customary international law. The protection of the rights of nonbelievers is one of the unfinished tasks of the United Nations. Although it is easy to overlook this issue, if nonbelievers do not feel that a future document of the United Nations will satisfy their convictions and protect their rights, their negative stance could inhibit any progress toward clarifying and strengthening the United Nations' position on the free exercise of religion.

In a significant book titled *Religion and Humane Global Governance,* Richard Falk of Princeton points to several reasons why religion can be useful, even indispensable, to developing a humane world scene. He points to contributions that have been made by religion through the ages, including fostering an appreciation of suffering, an ethos of solidarity, spiritual energy and nonviolent forms of struggle, and diverse ways of knowing desirable ways of reconciling science, reason, and spirituality.

Falk points out that the encouragement of the exercise of religion does not involve merely one person or one religious group engaging in prayer or worship. The activation of the spiritual energies of individuals or congregations can lead to very positive enrichments of society and the elevation of the public morality of a nation. For example, Falk opines that past efforts to outlaw slavery, colonization, and apartheid were "substantially inspired by direct and indirect religious thought as embodied in the lives and works of devout adherents" (32).

Falk concludes his comments on the usefulness of religious activities with these words: "The religious challenge is to infuse the struggles of the people of the world for democracy, equity, and sustainability with a vision of human existence that is human-centered yet conscious of the relevance of the sacred and of mysteries beyond the grasp of reason and machines" (33).

Those who are viscerally or philosophically opposed to efforts to advance organized religion must look objectively at what religious forces have accomplished in the past to bring about social justice. Before advocating any course that could unduly harm religion, opponents would do well to ponder the loss to the human family that would occur if religiously moti-

vated people were by national or international law discouraged or inhibited from fulfilling their faith-inspired desire to
act as Good Samaritans.

The Religious Freedom of Parents in Dissent

One of the greatest struggles for the freedom to dissent re-
volves around the religious orientation of the schools that
children attend. As they seek to educate their children properly, both believers and nonbelievers find the presence or absence of religious instruction in school curricula to be of para-
mount importance. Indeed, the subject can raise the question
whether government seeks to indoctrinate children in beliefs
that conflict with the beliefs of their parents. The matter understandably attracts great interest.

Boyle and Sheen's *Freedom of Religion and Belief* chronicles the state of religion in the major countries of the world
but includes little about how schools incorporate or neglect religion in their courses. Feelings on this topic tend to depend on
one's own educational background. Consequently, in the interests of full disclosure, let me state that I attended a Catholic
grade school for six years, taught mostly by nuns. I then went
to public schools in Massachusetts for junior and senior high
school, where the Bible was read to us daily. I graduated from
a Jesuit college.

Every nation and region of the Earth has a different opinion about the proper place of religion in schools. The subject
arouses the deepest passions of parents, religious officials, and
political authorities, but international law offers few guidelines. One of the reasons is the relative newness of the problem. Compulsory education was required at the national level
only in 1948, when the Universal Declaration of Human Rights

was issued. Thereafter, every new nation has had to establish some kind of mandatory education, but the number of children throughout the world who attend no school at all is still tragically high.

One underdeveloped issue involved in determining the proper place of religion in education is the right of parents to guide or even control the education of their children. Article 26 of the Universal Declaration of Human Rights states clearly that "parents have a prior right to choose the kind of education that shall be given to their children." It has never been fully clear what the word "prior" means in this context. The words chosen here were the result of compromises, accommodations, and the strong feelings of parents, especially religious ones, that they should have some right to decide the kind of schooling that their children would receive.

The UN Declaration on Religious Freedom of 1981 states that "every child shall enjoy the right to have access to education in the matter of religion or belief in accordance with the wishes of his parents." In addition, a child "shall not be compelled to receive teaching on religion or belief against the wishes of his parents or legal guardians." Decisional and statutory laws throughout Europe and elsewhere repeat these adages about the centrality of the rights of parents, but the implications are not always clear.

In the years after the collapse of communism, the countries formerly called "captive nations" struggled to locate the appropriate place of religion in their newly democratized societies. In 1990 the parliament of Hungary had a long debate on the question of restoring compulsory religious education in elementary and secondary schools, as had been required for decades before the takeover by the Communists. Ultimately, religious institutions were not restored to the public schools, but all of the political parties agreed that Hungary faced a moral crisis as to what values the government and the citizenry should accept and follow.

Many other nations have confronted the problems that Hungary faced. Outcomes vary, and because in each case only a single national government is making the crucial choice, little international law governing the roles and functions of parents' choice and the place of religion in the schools has emerged. Could international law evolve a bill of rights for parents as to the religious orientation of the schools their children attend? It is technically possible, but legislatures and courts have not yet evolved any internationally accepted way to integrate religion with education.

Perhaps the vastly disparate ways in which schools in various countries have developed make it unlikely that one ideal means to harmonize the teaching of religion with public education can be developed. This would be regrettable, because clearly the way government regulates religion in its common schools is of enormous importance to the question of the religious freedoms of both parent and child. Indeed, it seems safe to say that no other regulation about religion may be of such central importance.

A world survey of the church-state arrangements in respect to the place of religion in education reveals three common patterns:

1. A system in which separate church-related schools are subsidized. This system is common in England, in Europe, and in several of the Commonwealth nations.

2. An arrangement by which government allows the teaching of religion in or near the school premises but denies subsidies to nonpublic religiously affiliated schools. This is the system followed by the United States.
3. A school system that makes no accommodation to religious training and that does not allow separate schools sponsored by religious organizations. This system is employed in China.

These are not airtight classifications; some systems do not fit neatly within any single category. Furthermore, there is a surprising lack of literature about how these differing plans comport with generally accepted definitions of religious freedom or how they are compatible with internationally recognized parental rights. Nevertheless, I describe each of the three systems below.

Subsidized Private Schools

The first category of schools became reality in England around 1910 when the public or common school for the first time became a part of the English educational scheme. As the Church of England had no intention of abandoning its schools, England was compelled to recognize and fund Catholic and Jewish schools as well. In recent years, England, after long delays, has finally begun to fund Muslim schools also. The constitutionality of this arrangement has never been tested because England has no written constitution and no real judicial review of laws created by the parliament.

The system has made it possible for the large majority of

Catholic children to go to schools that are expressly religious and where regular courses in Catholicism are offered. Other religious groups have enjoyed the same privilege.

It is difficult to assess the effectiveness of this program. Do Catholics think that subsidized schools are the best way to carry out the instruction of their young constituents? Do they feel that their schools would have been more effective if they had more independence from the government?

This system has been accepted in England's former colonial empire, and it is still in use in countries such as India, Australia, Jamaica, and Canada. It has even spread beyond the Commonwealth nations and is the pattern in democracies such as Belgium and France. In fact, many supporters of church-related schools in the United States, arguing on behalf of subsidies for their own schools, point out that the United States is now the only democratic nation that denies subsidies to all church-related schools of less than collegiate rank. This may be so, but the differences between the United States and other countries are significant.

Parents in countries such as the Commonwealth nations can point to the United Nations documents that protect the rights of parents, but other issues are involved that deserve consideration. One of them is the fact that under the British system nonbelievers see their tax money go to subsidize and advance religious beliefs with which they disagree. Do agnostics or atheists have a right to feel aggrieved that their tax payments have been used to propagate beliefs they consider untrue or even dangerous? And if so, how do we weigh this perceived harm against the perceived good of advancing the religious freedom of parents who want their children to be educated in a setting where religion is not drowned out in a secular orientation? It is clear that both sets of parents have rights, but by what measure and by whom will they be evaluated and adjudicated?

Unsubsidized Private Schools, but Accommodating Public Schools

The second group of governments by tradition or law do not give subsidies to private schools but do make accommodations within the public schools for religious instruction. In Germany, Catholic and Lutheran students attend religious instruction given by accredited teachers in their public schools. There are excusal provisions, but they are rarely used. However, there are virtually no church-related schools in Germany. Crucifixes are displayed in the public schools in Catholic areas of Bavaria, but their presence has been contested.

Arrangements like the one in Germany can be found in several other countries. In such systems, the rights of parents are acknowledged, but could nonbelievers, acting under the norms of international law, have a legitimate complaint?

The United States can be placed in this second category, although it makes its facilities far less available than Germany does. The United States cannot be considered to be in the first group of countries, because it denies any subsidies to primary or secondary schools that are church-related, notwithstanding some incidental aids, such as free secular textbooks, bus rides, and certain health benefits. The possibility of the eventual availability of school vouchers, approved by a 5–4 decision of the U.S. Supreme Court in June 2002, remains very problematic.

But the United States does allow church-related religious education during the public school day if it is conducted off the school premises. In 1948, an 8–1 decision of the Supreme

Court disallowed programs of religious instruction conducted on public school premises even when parents agree to such programs in writing. The nationwide protest against this ruling may have been instrumental in the 1952 6–3 decision of *Zorach v. Clauson,* in which the Supreme Court allowed school districts to release pupils for religious instruction off school premises.

This program has not been utilized as widely as it could be. However, it is employed effectively in Utah, where public schools attended by large numbers of Mormon students have an efficient program whereby each school day students can go to nearby Mormon centers to receive instruction. Some non-Mormons feel that the system divides the school along sectarian lines, but the program is completely legal and is the Mormons' way of integrating their religion into the secular curricula of public schools.

But for the 48 million U.S. children attending public school in the United States, no religious teachings are to be had and no religious symbols are to be seen on school grounds during the school day. The alternative may be experienced by the approximately 5 million U.S. children attending private schools, over 2.5 million of whom go to Catholic schools. Another million U.S. children are now home-schooled, and thereby are the most influenced by the educational choices of their parents. The relatively new home-school movement has been created by parents who feel that their rights have been denied in the public schools; the core of this group is formed by active and articulate parents who protest the public schools because of their failure to offer religious instruction.

An amazing example of such parental protest can be found in the actions of some Amish parents in 1972, when in *Wisconsin v. Yoder* the Supreme Court allowed Amish parents to withdraw their children from high school. Amish parents wanted their children to be educated to a grade-school level of literacy, sufficient to read the Bible, but not beyond that level, lest they be tempted by secular knowledge and worldliness. The Supreme Court acknowledged these parents' right to raise their children in this manner and excused Amish children from laws requiring compulsory education through high school. The *Yoder* decision demonstrates the force of an appeal made by religious parents with strong conscientious objection to something that the state compels their children to undergo.

The United States is in a small group of nations that do not allow religious exercises in classrooms and deny any substantial assistance to private schools. It should be pointed out that in 1925 the U.S. Supreme Court unanimously sustained the right of private schools to exist. The people of Oregon, reacting to prejudice created in part by the Ku Klux Klan, voted in a plebiscite to forbid all private schools. The U.S. Supreme Court in *Pierce v. the Society of Sisters* set aside the results of the referendum and proclaimed the right of parents to establish and maintain nonpublic schools. The First Amendment to the U.S. Constitution was not involved because it had not yet been applied to the states via incorporation in the Fourteenth Amendment. The Court's ruling in *Pierce* bans any law that forbids the construction and operation of nonpublic schools.

Catholics and others in the United States have claimed that the government should provide subsidies for the secular aspects of Catholic schools. The petitions have failed in state legislatures, however, and, where successful, have been struck down by the courts.

Some observers feel that the denial of aid to Catholic schools is ultimately rooted in anti-Catholic bias, and their claim can be supported in part by history. In 1875, Senator James G. Blaine (R-Maine) introduced a constitutional amendment that would have prohibited aid for Catholic schools. It was supported by President Ulysses Grant and passed by the House of Representatives in a vote of 180 to 7. It failed to get the two-thirds vote needed to pass in the Senate. Several states enacted the essence of the Blaine amendment blocking aid for Catholic schools, but despite these obstacles, Catholic schools flourished. But the mentality behind the Blaine amendment was persistent in U.S. public opinion.

No case has yet been litigated in the United States in which Catholic parents attest that they could not *in conscience* send their child to any school where religion is not at the center of the curriculum—that to do so would be, for them, a sin. If parents could demonstrate this conscientious feeling, would the U.S. Supreme Court hold that they cannot be financially penalized for sending their children to a Catholic school? It is impossible to say, but at present the United States, rightly or wrongly, does not assist parents who want to send their children to schools that are religiously congruent with their faith and with the beliefs they want their children to learn in school.

In nations other than the United States, governments often work with cultural and religious groups to assist their schools. In Israel, for example, state-supported Muslim schools teach in Arabic. In India, nonpublic schools, including some 100 high schools and colleges operated by Jesuits, are subsidized. In Islamic nations, non-Muslim schools are rare but sometimes allowed. In these and other nations, the appeal of parental rights has been given at least some attention, although nowhere has the true depth of parental rights been realized or even examined.

Lack of Private Schools, Nonaccommodating Public Schools

Countries in the third category do not allow religion in their schools and do not permit private schools to exist. They could theoretically be charged with a violation of the religious freedom of the children involved and a denial of parental rights.

China is the largest of the nations in this category, although it should be pointed out that China has never had schools with a religious orientation; private schools are almost unknown. But China, in all its mystery and mysteriousness, calmly tells the world that parental rights are of little concern. By a long tradition in China, it is the sovereignty of the government that prevails and not the rights of parents. This can be seen in the Chinese denial to most parents of the right to have a second or third child. China's policy is similar to those of the other Communist nations that existed from 1950 to 1990, where religion was not taught or even mentioned in public schools and where private schools were generally not allowed.

Could international law develop so that no nation could forbid private schools if they are the result of parental demands for religious freedom? Perhaps, but it is easy to see that the right of religiously oriented parents to choose the schools their children attend has not developed in the way that certain other personal rights have flowered.

The Declaration on Religious Freedom agreed to by the United Nations General Assembly in 1981 strongly urges that a person's religion or belief is "one of the fundamental elements in his conception of life and that freedom of religion or belief should be fully respected and guaranteed." It goes on to forbid "the use of religion or belief for ends inconsistent with the charter of the United Nations."

The protection of the rights of parents and their children is part of the objective announced in the declaration. Article 5 mandates in broad terms that parents "have the right to organize the life within the family in accordance with their religion or belief." They have a right to expect that government will respect the "moral education in which they believe the child should be brought up."

In the vast literature about religious freedom and international law, there are very few references to the rights of parents with regard to deciding the education of their children. One of the reasons, of course, is the dominant position many governments take in the cultural and religious life of their countries. In Indonesia, for example, everyone is required to state his or her religion on a government-issued identity card; children cannot enter school without a statement of their religion.

The absence of concern about the rights of parents also derives from the traditional disregard by sovereign states of the personal individual rights of citizens. This is one of the major reasons why the international community after World War II revolted against the arrogance and omnipotence of individual nations and created international standards that sovereign nations could not avoid or deny. But this new world attitude recognizing individual human rights that can sometimes trump the will of the state has yet to translate to expanded rights for parents. It may be that a whole new jurisprudence on the status of parents is about to be born.

Implicit in the definitions and determinations of the rights of parents is the global awakening to the rights of children. The Covenant on the Rights of the Child (CRC) contains commitments to children that were hardly heard of before the United Nations passed it in 1989. It does not spell out a child's right to receive adequate information about the religions of the world, but there may now be a feeling that children should not be deprived of knowledge of religions other than their own.

Some observers will suggest that this idea is unrealistic, and that no state, much less the international community, should interfere in the delicate and highly personal area of teaching religion to one's children. In fact, the United Nations documents about parents and the rights of children assume that the parents are in control and can transmit to their offspring the religion of their choice or no religion at all. But the 1981 Declaration on Religious Freedom points out that the "disregard and infringement of human rights and fundamental freedoms have brought directly or indirectly wars and great suffering to humankind" and have kindled "hatred between peoples and nations."

The international community certainly has an interest in preventing the rise of "hatred between peoples and nations." Is such a "kindling" going on in the religious instructions given by certain Christian, Islamic, and other religious entities? Are political authorities using their countries' religious institutions to promote hatred and animosity among children?

The literature on comparative religions observes that all major faiths are centered on the idea of human dignity and the duty to love all of God's sons and daughters. This is the essence of the traditional and unanimous message of all religions. How could some religions through history have gone so far astray from their core message?

Could it be that a world authority will eventually be created with the right and the duty to tell religious persons that they cannot preach something that contravenes international law? The preamble of the United Nations Declaration on Religious Freedom reminds nations that they cannot use "religion or beliefs for ends inconsistent with the charter of the United Nations." To achieve this objective, it is essential that nations

"promote understanding, tolerance and respect in matters related to freedom of religion and belief."

In reading the 500 pages of Boyle and Sheen's *Freedom of
Religion and Belief,* one is surprised to recognize that even the
best authorities know little about the status of religion in the
world. Millions of people fear and even loathe organized religion and do not want to see it encouraged or recognized. They
feel that, in the words of the Universal Declaration of Human
Rights, religion has kindled "hatred between peoples and nations." Their worst fears have been confirmed by the ethnic and
religious savageries in the Balkans and in Rwanda.

However, this fear and suspicion can go too far. It is sometimes difficult for those who are bluntly opposed to organized
religion to recognize the civilizing and elevating influence that
religion has had through the ages. The creation of beautiful art
and music that has been fostered by organized religions can be
obscured by the savage uses to which political leaders have put
religion for their own horrendous objectives. As important as
it is that the world acknowledge the past transgressions committed in the name of religion, it is also crucial that no one forget the many benefits that have been derived from organizations of faith.

The United Nations Declaration on Religious Freedom is
an attempt to spell out in one document the subtle inter-
connections between religion and government. It is a laudable
endeavor, and it does make an effort to speak to the rights of
parents in connection with the religious upbringing of their
children. The end product may be incomplete, but it is the result of the nations of the Earth wondering, really for the first
time in history, how governments, parents, and children should
regard the proper place of religion. The declaration may not
fully resolve this profound question, but it is a noble beginning.

VIII

Religious Freedom and Issues of Gender and Sexuality

V iolations of religious freedom affect individuals, families, and communities. However, this refusal to abide by international law has a particular impact on the rights of two distinct groups who have only recently begun to share in the universal promise of equality: women and homosexuals.

Women

The emergence of the feminist movement since the 1960s has coincided with the development of international human rights. Women have benefited enormously in claiming the equality that international law confirms is rightfully theirs, but their progress has been slowed by the pervasiveness of the institutions that have subordinated women for centuries. Indeed, the repression of women over past centuries has been continuous and fierce.

It is surprising that there is such a small body of literature about the role that international law should play in reforming religious principles that affect the status granted to women. In the United States and Europe, governmental law has sought to bring equality to women in the jobs they hold, the estates they inherit, and the ways they control their child-bearing. Some of the rules articulated by the world's major religions, however, continue to subordinate women. They have been mitigated or moderated in some countries, but some practices of this kind may result, directly or indirectly, from the traditional domination of men over women in many, if not all, societies.

Of course, some practices have been utterly discredited; one could point to the new awareness of and protection against female genital mutilation. However, this abuse of young women is clearly not called for by the Muslim religion, but rather is the result of a combination of myths and misrepresentations perpetuated by men for the alleged benefit of men.

An emerging and difficult question is whether a set of rights for women clarified and enriched by international law can or should trump the right of religious groups to practice their beliefs. The almost inviolable right to the free exercise of religion, and particularly the right to follow conscience, presumably extends to religious groups that embrace beliefs that subordinate women. An obvious example is the refusal of the Catholic Church and other religious bodies to ordain women as priests. Should international law require that, despite the sincerely held views of the leaders of the Catholic Church, women must be given the opportunity to be ordained?

U.S. law, if it had to decide this question, would hold that neither national nor international law can require a religion to change practices that it bases on sincerely held religious views. Of course, there are exceptions; for example, U.S. law does not allow a religion to deny blood transfusions to minors or to sanction the mistreatment of persons who refuse to convert.

But exceptions of this kind do not help a woman who feels harmed because her church follows a creed that denies her benefits or status because of her gender.

This tension between religious rights and women's rights highlights one reason that the architects of international human rights have not given to the freedom of religion the same vigorous attention they have bestowed on the elimination of torture, the guarantee of a free press, and the development of the rights of children. Of course, international law should be more attentive to the right to religious freedom—but the past and continuing persecution of women suggests that the proper balance between deference to religion and recognition of women's rights has not yet been reached.

For centuries religious groups have been imposing limitations and restrictions on women as a class. Almost always the restrictions are based on the belief that women have fewer, or at least different, rights than men. And the men who impose such standards sincerely believe that God has revealed that he desires and demands that such restrictions be imposed on women.

The global revolution for human rights begun with the Universal Declaration of Human Rights helped to spark a revolution for the rights of women. It is impossible to overstate the enormity of the awakening in the consciousness of women concerning their equality and their rights. This new awareness after centuries of slumber is almost certainly irreversible. It is not directly aimed at any of the world's religions, but the leaders in the worldwide movement to obtain rights for women have to know that some of the inequalities that women experience derive directly or indirectly from doctrines formulated by leaders of Judaism, Christianity, and the other major religions.

Advocates in the international women's movement have met in large numbers in Mexico City, Nairobi, and Beijing.

These activists do not openly state that they are asking for a reversal or a setting aside of the teachings of religion. However, they do assert that religious tenets that require women to be denied rights accorded to men must ultimately yield to the human rights revolution in international law. For their part, the major religions have increasingly recognized that they will eventually have to confront and resolve the demands placed before them by the world's women.

It is generally assumed that if women voluntarily convert to a religion or choose to continue as members of a religious denomination, they accept the ordinances of that group, even though men and women may be treated unequally. However, this seemingly simple presumption runs into great trouble when the religious body in question seeks to impose its views on the civil law of a nation. The pattern is familiar; for example, Catholic officials in Ireland, Jewish authorities in Israel, and Muslim leaders in Saudi Arabia all seek to transmit their religious views into the civil legal system. In such cases, women may be constrained by secular standards of inequality drawn from a religion they may or may not follow. Moreover, even when women choose to continue with a religion that treats them unequally, they may still claim that the disabilities placed on them are in violation of the guarantees of religious freedom that are a firm part of the world law of human rights.

The status historically granted to women by the major religions is well known, and it seems to have been generally accepted before the birth of the international human rights revolution after World War II. The generally subordinate status of women in the world of religion may have started in what is still the position of Orthodox Judaism. In that faith, women are not counted as part of a minion, or the minimum number of people needed to conduct a religious service. They are not permitted to be rabbis, their evidence is not acceptable in court, and, unlike men, they cannot obtain a divorce against their spouse's will. The unequal and undesirable position of women is even recognized within the prayers of Judaism, as each Orthodox Jewish man in his daily morning prayer thanks God for not having made him a woman. Jewish spokesmen claim, of course, that their faith holds women's position as different than but not inferior to that of men. Of course, Catholic and Muslim traditions impose comparable disabilities on women.

The partisans and defenders of the world's organized religions may insist that the subordination of women has been a part of every civilization since the beginning of recorded history and that religions have simply accepted that reality. This may be true to some extent, but the contemporary feminist revolution, which first flowered in the 1960s and 1970s, seeks to eliminate the continued stereotyping and subordination of women by religions in the modern world.

Is there an open conflict between the mandates of the Convention on the Elimination of Discrimination against Women (CEDAW) and the 1981 United Nations Declaration on Religious Freedom? If so, which point of view should prevail? Sincere men—and indeed some women—involved in organized religion will claim that God himself has established the teachings by which Judaism, Christianity, and Islam assign the status and rights of women. If they continue to maintain this position, international law will have to make a judgment as to whether the convictions held because of a religious faith should trump near-universal modern convictions on the equality of men and women. Of course, it is possible that religious adherents will eventually reexamine their convictions in light of modern standards and decide that they have misinterpreted their revelations from God. This has happened before;

for example, some religious bodies eventually eased their resistance to female suffrage after women obtained the vote in the United States in 1920.

Alternately, governments could insist on a change of view by the established religions, as was the case when the United States Congress insisted that the practice of polygamy had to be banned before Utah could achieve statehood. Although Mormons believed that God had revealed to them that polygamy was their right and in fact their duty if they had the means to practice it, their leaders eventually yielded. Such governmental action, however, is very rare; the case of polygamy is probably the only clear example in U.S. history in which the government insisted that a religious group could not act in accord with a belief they thought to be revealed by God.

Is it possible that world authorities, pursuant to widespread public opinion, will ban polygamy as being inherently degrading to women? It seems certain that some Muslim authorities would claim that it is a divine decree that some men be able to practice polygamy. However, the humiliation forced upon plural wives is so clear that one must conclude that this issue will eventually draw the attention of international law.

But in other areas, there does not appear to be any major change in the religious status of women on the horizon. The alienation of millions of women from Judaism, Christianity, and Islam may put pressure on those groups to rethink their traditional positions on women, but even if it does not, the struggle of women within these religions raises an issue of religious freedom in international law. All members of faith-based organizations, whether espousing orthodox ideas on the status of women or new interpretations, want definite commitments from international human rights law that they will be able to hold firm to their convictions.

Is it possible that some reconciliation between women's

aspirations and traditional religious bodies can be arrived at? The subordination of women has become so ingrained and accepted in society that it seems difficult to expect a radical change in a short time. One could argue that the status of women in many areas of the world—especially in countries outside the Judeo-Christian world—is due more to historical and cultural attitudes than to religious beliefs.

But the CEDAW—ratified by the vast majority of nations but not by the United States—makes no explicit exception for inequalities imposed on women because of religious beliefs. The CEDAW condemns all of the handicaps and disabilities that women have inherited from the centuries during which they were treated by custom and by law as inferior, or at least subordinate, to men. Indeed, in May 2001 the UN Committee on CEDAW concluded that polygamy violates Article 5(a) of the convention: "Polygamous marriage contravenes a woman's right to equality with men, and can have such serious emotional and financial consequences for her and her dependents that such marriages ought to be discouraged and prohibited."

The open persecution of disfavored religions in such nations as China, Afghanistan, and Sudan may continue. The silent but ferocious wars against women will continue in scores of other countries on premises that derive not only from religious customs but also from the sheer age-old domination of women by men.

Millions of women will continue to protest. But the millions of other women who adhere to the religions that discriminate against them may accept their unequal status on the basis that God has ordained it. For their part, the leaders of these religious groups will continue to stress their belief that their religions' teachings on the status of women have been revealed by God. The result may be, to some extent, a standoff.

Of course, some religious leaders and groups may modify their position on women. They may well conclude that the dominant position held by men in some religions was inherited from pagan, male-dominated societies and is not a part of the sacred revelations of God.

There is also the distinct possibility that Christian women will search Church traditions and prove that their subordinate status is inconsistent with the authentic teachings of the Bible and the doctrines of Christ. The struggle of women in the Catholic Church to obtain the right to be ordained to the priesthood is certainly based on the search for a new and revised interpretation of the Scriptures and of tradition. These women and their supporters might also employ an argument based on religious freedom; they could well assert that international law entitles them to equality in their religious allegiance—unless that equality is clearly denied by an indisputable teaching revealed by God.

The essays collected by Courtney W. Howland in *Religious Fundamentalists and the Human Rights of Women* illustrate the struggle of women for equality in all of the major religious bodies of the world. In the book's twenty-seven chapters the reader sees the unequal results of the application to women of certain Jewish, Christian, Islamic, and Buddhist principles and traditions. Evidence of domestic violence, arranged marriages, denial of schooling to girls, and female genital mutilation demonstrates the cruelty and inequality imposed on women often, but not always, in the name of religion.

Howland argues that the abuses he records constitute an evisceration of religion, and therefore are not privileged as exercises of religious freedom. The volume implicitly calls for the creation of an international monitoring group akin to the six United Nations committees that currently monitor nation-states' compliance with the obligations they have assumed under various treaties.

The Howland collection concentrates on fundamentalists among religious bodies. These persons are identified as strict, literal interpreters of religious traditions. A comparable study on this group is *The Fundamentalist Project: Fundamentalism and Society,* by Martin Marty and R. Appleby. It seems fair to state that the fundamentalists in religious circles adhere strictly to the literal text of what they perceive to be their mandate. The topic is vast, and the discussion of fundamentalism has taken on a pejorative tone. But again, the international law on religious freedom does not judge the claims of literals and liberals. In other words, if a religious group holds a strictly traditionalist view of the place of women, international law does not lightly seek to deprive it of the capacity to follow a practice that, in its judgment, comes from the Creator and must be obeyed in conscience.

Studies in fundamentalism have made clear the diversity of opinion among religious groups concerning the proper place and status of women. The Koran has long been interpreted by male scholars, but feminist theologians are now arriving at new insights. The proper positions of women in the Hindu and Buddhist traditions are also being reexamined. It is possible that the global explosion of concern for the rights of women could overcome the widespread resistance to any change in the position of women. Yet the stereotyped position considered appropriate to women is so entrenched that it may take generations to eradicate.

No issue related to the global rights of women has surfaced more dramatically than the subject of female genital mutilation. In several nations, largely in Africa, the custom of forcing girls around the age of twelve to undergo painful surgery that will prevent them from having intercourse with a man before marriage has persisted for centuries. The origins of this barbarous procedure are unknown. It is practiced in several Islamic countries, although whether it stems from the Koran is in dispute. Some countries, such as Egypt, have tried to outlaw the practice, and all medical organizations have condemned it as worthless and indeed harmful.

In at least one case, the United States granted asylum to a woman who was threatened with genital mutilation in her country of origin. The court held that female genital mutilation is a form of torture—a practice absolutely prohibited by international law. An abundant and growing body of literature on female genital mutilation almost universally condemns the practice. This is a case in which, even if Islamic belief sanctioned the practice, the law of international human rights would firmly condemn and prohibit it. Are there other beliefs, traditions, and practices injurious to women that would also merit condemnation? There probably are, although it is difficult to imagine that they could be as savage and indefensible as female genital mutilation.

Will practices that humiliate and degrade women on the basis of some religious belief be challenged as incompatible with the rapidly expanding body of international human rights law? It is possible, but there is as yet no tribunal to which claims based on religious freedom can be referred. However, there is a UN committee on women, created to monitor signatories' compliance with CEDAW. There is some evidence that this committee is prepared to go out of its way to condemn practices that clearly violate the religious freedom of women. Although feeble, this machinery reviews the conduct of nations and announces those practices it deems to be detrimental to the equality and religious freedom of women.

The optional protocol allowing women to report their grievances directly to the UN committee on CEDAW entered into force on December 22, 2000. However, there is a massive reluctance in that body and elsewhere to investigate religious entities and charge them with violations of religious freedom. Faith-based organizations receive a great deal of deference due to the assumption that their purpose is to assist their members' search for the will of the Almighty. Even when the dictates and practices of religious bodies seem to collide with assumed maxims of good law and behavior, they are ordinarily granted forbearance because of their spiritual or theistic motivations.

More vulnerable is the theory of cultural relativity—the belief that different cultures are generally entitled to pursue their own traditions and customs even when they appear to be in conflict with international standards. This argument used to be advanced regarding female genital mutilation, but such a contention seems to be fading away.

Of course, many religious groups are proactive on the rights of women, and the feeling of solidarity among women regarding their dignity, equality, and human rights has increased exponentially. Perhaps the seriousness with which women confront challenges to their equality will prompt male religious leaders to reexamine their treatment of women and their interpretations of their religions' teachings about the role of women. While corporations and governments have successfully expanded the rights of women, churches have had mixed results. A reading of CEDAW and the rulings of the UN committee that monitors its effectiveness might convince religious leaders that their organizations will be left behind if they do not pay heed to women's claims to human rights.

However, one should not assume that the feminist organizations operating in Europe and the United States will soon persuade the leaders of nations traditionally backward on the rights of women to grant them equality and partnership. These organizations would have a much better chance if they could demonstrate that the rights they are struggling to attain are not really denied by the major domestic religious bodies. But the religious leaders who could confirm such claims often benefit from the corporate support of entrenched governments, which are not eager to see political power pass to their female citizens.

Although a convention on religious freedom, rather than a mere UN declaration, would be desirable, it should be noted that the nations that have signed and ratified the International Covenant on Cultural and Political Rights (ICCPR) have accepted an affirmative obligation to make available the religious freedom granted in the covenant. Each signatory has assumed the obligations to "ensure" religious freedom and to adopt laws and other measures against private interference with the enjoyment of the right to religious freedom guaranteed in ICCPR. Of course, even if countries live up to their obligations and take affirmative measures to provide religious freedom, there will still always be religious difficulties. The relationship of church and state was a thorny problem both before and after Christ told his listeners to render to God what is God's and to Caesar what is Caesar's.

The role of the government toward religion is further complicated by the patriarchal attitudes assumed by religious leaders centuries ago. The dominant role held by males in churches no doubt made further patriarchy seem natural. Indeed, most unelected leaders in history—especially religious ones—have been authoritarian, even autocratic, as well as benignly patriarchal. The attitude has been so pervasive and permanent that religious leaders seem to have adopted it by instinct.

But all generalizations about the appropriate place of

women in society and in churches are probably living on borrowed time. The place of women will almost certainly change more in the next few generations than in all previous centuries. Even in the remote villages of India where 400 million people reside in backward and even primitive situations, women's aspirations for equality can be found. And this hope for a world where women are not second to men is reinforced by faith. In other words, women the world over can use their religious beliefs to reach the inexorable conclusion that men should not have power over them. While all women may not hear the feminist rhetoric of the West, they know that there is something outdated and wrong in the teaching that women are born to be second-rate servants of men.

It is difficult to understand why, despite the emergence of democracy in the nineteenth century and the birth of international human rights in the twentieth century, there is still such a profound division between men and women, with men as the dominant partners, as always through history, in deciding public policy, the objectives of society, and the parameters of marriage. Could the religions of the world gradually emancipate women, insisting on religious freedom for everyone and making gender rights the moral center of the twenty-first century? That question is more complex and bothersome than any issue in the whole catalog of topics involved in the human rights revolution.

Abortion

Another difficult issue on which an internationally binding ruling is forthcoming is abortion. Convictions run strong on the question of when, if ever, the government can allow a woman to terminate her pregnancy. The point claimed by some feminists is clear: a woman has the unconditional right to end her pregnancy, at very least within the first trimester. The counterpoint is made by religious groups that would deny the woman that right at any time.

It is not clear whether laws regulating pregnancy are really enforceable. It is estimated that some 40 million abortions are performed each year in the world. At least 1.4 million abortions are performed annually in the United States; that means that roughly every third pregnancy in the United States ends in abortion. Whether the force of law could effectively stem that tide is unknown. Legal bans on abortion in the West are increasingly rare; they exist in Ireland, Portugal, and Chile. Islamic nations deter abortions, whereas China requires it in some cases.

Women who are denied an abortion in some nations can claim that their convictions that derive from "religion or belief" have not been respected. But to many others, that claim is not self-evident. Eventually an international tribunal may conclude that, absent the most serious threat to the life or health of the mother, international law guarantees the unborn child's right to life.

This issue obviously highlights a clash of fundamental views about the value of life, the rights of pregnant women, and the message sent to society by the availability of abortion. Is it possible that if the difficult issue of abortion ever came before a United Nations decision-making body, such a panel could rule that a potential human life must be held as indestructible, such that no nation could allow its termination? If such a ruling ever did emerge, it would come from a global forum after the most vigorous pro-life and pro-choice advocates had argued their clashing positions. One religious worldview would have prevailed over another.

The specter of such a ruling might cause many observers to withdraw to the position that certain complicated moral priorities should be resolved at the local level. But such a position is probably unrealistic, as globalization in all its forms is almost inevitable. Emotional issues related to religion and faith cannot for long escape rulings or regulations that are binding across the globe.

Some will urge a certain cultural relativism that allows local variations on world norms. As we have seen, when the practice of female genital mutilation in some African nations came to world attention, it was initially suggested that this might represent a legitimate instance of cultural relativism. But the barbarity of the practice ultimately led to the widely held view that no cultural practice of such an indefensible nature could escape the scrutiny of international norms on human rights. Clearly, international jurists and specialists on human rights will continue to raise such questions about practices sanctioned by governments or carried out by private groups that are offensive to recognized norms of acceptable conduct, and thereby cry out for international regulation. Whether the issue of abortion will fall under such attention and what the outcome would be remains to be seen.

Homosexuals

The legal rights of homosexuals will ultimately have to be resolved by some international authority. Pleas by the gay community for equal treatment raised in the courts and in the legislatures deserve and demand resolution. To date, the success of the gay community in advancing its rights has been uneven: the legalization of gay civil unions in Vermont and gay marriages in Massachusetts will apparently not be replicated soon in other states, and the victories for the gay community in the European Court of Human Rights (ECHR) are significant but by no means a complete vindication of the rights that they claim. For example, the ECHR, in Strasbourg, has ruled that Northern Ireland may not enforce its nearly dormant laws criminalizing sodomy, but the status of gays, whether alone or living with a partner, remains unsettled in national and international law.

If some individuals are convinced in their conscience that they were born homosexual and must live in the way that God created them, should there be some international guarantee that prohibits nations from discriminating against them? The answer has to be yes, but how? The ECHR's decision on Northern Ireland's sodomy law was binding because the United Kingdom in the early 1950s agreed to be bound by the rulings of the ECHR. If Christian, Muslim, or other nations ratified a covenant guaranteeing religious freedom, they would be similarly bound by their commitment. However, Muslim nations, and perhaps some others, would almost certainly place reservations on their commitment to the treaty based on their strong convictions against any legal approval of the practice of homosexuality.

In the United States a broad phalanx of religious organizations are vigorously opposed to almost any legal vindication of the practice of homosexuality. While it is clear that religious fundamentalists will sometimes exaggerate the meaning of biblical statements concerning homosexuality, many mainstream religions similarly oppose legal recognition of homosexuals and lesbians. For example, such groups often oppose the granting of pension or health benefits to gay partners. The issue of AIDS only complicates religious thinking and feeling on this topic.

But the claims of the gay community, so far as they are based on religion or belief, arguably fit within the protection of the guarantees of religious freedom coined in the 1981 United Nations Declaration on Religious Freedom. At the very least, when their religious claims are ignored by domestic legislatures and courts, members of the gay community deserve an international forum in which to bring their claims that their countries of residence have improperly denied them relief.

These claims of homosexuals are relatively new on the world scene, and it is not clear that an international tribunal would agree with them. But in denying these sought-after liberties, the members of any such international panel would have to demonstrate that the religious beliefs of the gay community called for practices that sovereign nations can properly ban. It is not clear, however, that the parties contending for the legal place of gays would want to try their case in a world forum. Both gays and governments would fear losing their claim in the most public way. Moreover, the ruling could be so opaque as to provide no clarity on the legal status of the religious freedoms claimed or on the right of governments to curb homosexual rights.

The whole theory behind observing internationally recognized religious rights is based on the understanding that nations can be governed by antireligious factions or groups under the strong influence of specific denominations. In either case, the result can be government suppression of religious practices. Certainly this risk is amplified when the minority religious view being challenged is linked to homosexual conduct, but the complexity of the legal claims is also vastly increased. There does seem to be a consensus that the availability of a world tribunal on religion is a good idea, but how can such a tribunal be expected to have the wisdom of a Solomon?

IX

When Governments Repress
and Persecute Religion

Some nations embrace religious pluralism and allow nearly unrestricted speech by religious groups or organizations of conscience. In the United States, for example, the peace community would complain that they had been gagged if the government pressured them to cease their vigorous claims that the government is excessively belligerent and warlike. Organizations such as Pax Christi, a near pacifist group made up predominantly of Catholics, would clearly claim an infringement of their religious freedom if the U.S. government sought to discredit their views and disallow their activities. This domestic religious liberty, however, stems largely from provisions in the U.S. Constitution rather than from the demands of international law. Clearly, many nations are not so tolerant of voices of conscience. Members of repressed religious groups in those nations look to international law to set and monitor minimum standards of religious liberty. But what is the state of international law regarding religious repression?

The world scene where religious groups and governments vie for ascendancy can suggest that there is no legal or
international process by which clashes of this kind can be regulated. Indeed, that there was no such process was the accepted
truth for many centuries before the establishment of the United
Nations and its human rights commissions. It is now understood that no nation can expect to escape punishment if it en-
gages in serious misconduct in repressing the internationally
recognized human rights of its citizens.

However, a nation's accountability for abuse of the religious rights of its citizenry is legally one step below its accountability for violations of political and economic rights. While
the latter rights are protected by UN covenants, the guarantee
of religious freedom is protected only by a UN declaration.
The United Nations' ability to ensure compliance with covenants on human rights is far from satisfactory, but it has even
less power to question whether nations' actions are consistent
with declared aspirations for religious freedom. As a result, there
is an urgent need to create some kind of juridical supervision
of the conduct of nations that brutally repress the activities of
religious bodies. One such nation was El Salvador, which, beginning in 1987, killed seventeen priests, one archbishop, and
thousands of religious laypeople in an effort to extirpate the
values taught by these Catholics. A review of these events is
instructive.

The first priest to be murdered in this campaign was Father Rutilio Grande, a Jesuit, who, as the president of the Priests'
Senate in El Salvador, was the most visible clergyman in the
small country of five million people. The government took
the open position that the priests had adopted a version of the
Gospels and an interpretation of the documents of Vatican II

that was "subversive" of the government. Father Grande paid
for such dissent with his life.

On November 16, 1989, the unelected government of El
Salvador sought to put even greater force behind its belief by
murdering six Jesuits who operated the University of Central
America when that institution, along with the Jesuits, was
declared to be subversive. The brutal details of how soldiers
dragged the Jesuits out of their home and slaughtered them at
2:00 a.m. in their garden along with their housekeeper and her
daughter is known worldwide.

The murders were committed for reasons that were specifically religious: the government wanted to suppress the dissemination of religious principles. This was the same objective
behind the earlier assassination of Archbishop Oscar Romero
as he was saying mass on March 24, 1980. The same antireligious
principle was operating in the murder of four American churchwomen in December 1980.

The carnage carried out in El Salvador by a government
in the name of repressing a religion is possibly the best-known
instance in recent history of an open attempt to annihilate a
religion. There have obviously been similar situations around
the world, but the tragic occurrences in El Salvador—in which
the United States played a major role—challenge the international community to create legal machinery that will punish
and deter such events.

Rights of all kinds guaranteed by world law were violated
in El Salvador. The United Nations eventually brought about
an armistice of sorts, but virtually no remedies were decreed
for the victims. The University of Central America received no
indemnity for the murder of its six Jesuit professors. There was
no relief or reparation for the families of the 75,000 people

who had been killed in a civil war between a government armed by the United States and peasants crying out for social justice. This war, with its carnage, was possibly more about religion than any other modern war of its kind, but international law was then, and remains today, silent and impotent on the matter.

One remedy, however, was available to some victims in El Salvador—one based not primarily on a violation of religious freedom but on the acts of torture carried out by two generals and the security forces of El Salvador. On July 22, 2002, a federal jury in West Palm Beach, Florida, awarded $54.6 million in damages to three civilians who had been tortured twenty years earlier by Salvadorian military officers who had since come to Florida. The jury accepted the victims' graphic testimony of beatings, gang rapes, and other forms of torture. The Torture Victim Protection Act (TVPA), enacted by the U.S. Congress in 1992, authorized the court to award damages for torture committed abroad in violation of international law. The enactment and enforcement of this law is a rare instance in which one nation, recognizing that an act is forbidden by world law, has embraced its obligation to carry out the world's legal ban of that act.

The verdict against the two generals brought special satisfaction to the families of the 75,000 Salvadorians slain in the war. A truth commission in El Salvador concluded that the military and its allied death squads were responsible for 85 percent of the abuses committed during the conflict. Moreover, the Florida verdict brought relief because the plaintiffs had failed to persuade an earlier jury that the same two generals were responsible for the deaths of the four American churchwomen slain in El Salvador in 1980. The three plaintiffs in that case— a church worker, a physician, and a professor—had all been motivated directly or indirectly by the theology of Vatican II, which earlier had played a very prominent role in the struggle of Catholics against the tyranny of El Salvador's government.

In April 2002 Amnesty International estimated that there were some 1,000 suspected torturers in the United States. Victims can sue them under the Alien Tort Claims Act passed by the first Congress in 1789 and updated with the TVPA in 1992. But the denial of religious freedom does not currently give rise to a claim that is cognizable under international law. At the moment, the United States provides no way for victims to sue anyone who has denied them religious freedom in another country.

If the denial of religious freedom were accepted as a violation of international law, as torture is, could the United States and other nations put persons who have denied religious liberty on trial like the torturers? Someday—perhaps soon—the answer may be yes. If the United Nations Declaration on Religious Freedom were elevated to the status of a covenant, it would be ratified by most nations and thus become a vehicle for the punishment of people such as the generals in El Salvador who sought to crush a version of Catholicism that, in their view, undermined their government.

Many nations recognize their lack of adequate means to enforce the right to religious freedom, but few take action. In 1993 Belgium enacted a law designed to reach dictators and despots. The law confers on Belgian courts jurisdiction for certain human rights abuses, even if the crime was not committed on Belgian soil. To date, however, the only people convicted under the law were four Rwandans brought to trial for their role in the genocide of members of the Tutsi tribe by Hutu militiamen in 1994. Human rights cases filed against Fidel Castro, Yasser Arafat, Saddam Hussein, and several African leaders were all dismissed because the defendants were not physically present in Belgium. Charges of war crimes against Ariel Sharon of Israel were also set aside.

The International Criminal Court (ICC), which came into operation on July 1, 2002, may be able to take up some of these cases, although its jurisdiction is limited to charges involving genocide, crimes against humanity, and crimes of war. In addition, the ICC is hampered by the widely criticized refusal of the United States to be bound by the treaty and its insistence that the UN Security Council give immunity to all U.S. military personnel during the first year of the court's operation.

It is sad to think that, except for the TVPA in the United States and the new legal machinery in Belgium, there are hardly any laws offering victims of serious religious intolerance injunctive or compensatory relief. Even the European Court of Human Rights (ECHR) in Strasbourg does not seem to be offering much hope for religious minorities who suffer intolerance in Europe.

The lack of sensitivity of some European nations to certain minority religious groups is, of course, minor compared to the onslaught against religion in El Salvador. But the lack of tolerance in Europe suggests the need for a higher sensitivity to religion and for a commission or tribunal to hear the grievances of persons who feel that the government is telling them to do something that their faith and their conscience tell them not to do.

The thought that tolerance of religious groups is growing appears to be overoptimistic. The book *The Catholic Martyrs of the Twentieth Century,* by Robert Royal, indicates that there was more persecution of religion in the twentieth century than in any previous century. The number of persons incarcerated in the name of religion is staggering when one considers that the United Nations, with its guarantees of religious freedom, was established before the century was half over. It is therefore wise to accept the sobering reality that the harassment of religious groups by governmental and other religious entities may be inevitable. But there is some reason to hope that the international human rights revolution may diminish the likelihood that people and nations will act out of hatred toward people and organizations founded on faith in God.

One can see terrible instances of the hatred of religion in non-Christian countries such as China as well as in Christian nations such as El Salvador. What is the state of religious freedom in the countries of Europe—clearly the oldest Christian nations in the world? A certain religious tranquility has come to European society. But the eldest daughters of the Catholic Church are still groping with the challenges of what Europe pejoratively calls "cults."

The rise of new religious movements in Europe has brought forth scores of articles on the origins and meanings of this unusual phenomenon. Some observers theorize that the rise of secularism all over Europe has prompted young people to opt for some form of faith that responds to their need for a spiritual explanation of the mystery of existence. The traditional forms of Catholicism and Protestantism are seemingly losing some of their appeal for generations born many years after World War II.

These new sects have frightened many Europeans. Some new religious groups are accused of brainwashing and even kidnapping. In January 1996 a French national commission on cults blacklisted 172 organizations, among them Southern Baptists, Opus Dei, Seventh-Day Adventists, Jehovah's Witnesses, and Scientologists. No precise definition of a "cult" was issued by the French government, but the listing clearly marginalized members of these organizations.

In May 2001 France passed a law that allows for the dissolution of certain religious organizations, recognizes a cause of action for "mental manipulation," and limits proselytizing. The literature about the new anticult atmosphere continues to grow, and France's anticult strategy has inhibited many religious groups. The most vocal and visible opposition to the so-called cults comes from the families of children who have been caught up in the secret atmosphere of the new and sometimes clandestine religions.

Other nations have taken different measures. Belgium has not enacted anticult legislation but has produced a blacklist of 189 religious organizations and created an agency to monitor them. Belgium has expelled religious workers of the Assembly of God. Germany has also established a commission to monitor cults, and Germany's refusal to recognize the Church of Scientology is well known. Whether Germany's declaration that Scientology is not a religion insulates it from the charge that it is denying Scientologists religious freedom is a matter for discussion.

The Parliament of the European Union has expressed the view that existing criminal laws contain sufficient sanctions to counter any unlawful activity by cults, so no special measures need be taken. This decision suggests that France, Belgium, and Germany may have overreacted to the emergence of cults.

The legitimacy of anticult initiatives may ultimately be decided by the ECHR. Article 9 of the European Convention on Human Rights protects the "freedom to manifest one's religion or belief," and this right is "subject only to such limitations as are prescribed by law and are necessary in a democratic society in the interest of public safety, for the protection of public order, health or morals, or for the protection of the rights and freedoms of others."

In the first claim on religion heard by the ECHR, the 1993 case of *Kokkinakis v. Greece,* the tribunal held that Greece's antiproselytizing law could not be upheld when it was used against a Jehovah's Witness who spoke to the wife of a cantor of the Greek Orthodox Church. In terms very sympathetic to the objectives of the Greek law prohibiting proselytizing, the ECHR ruled that the conviction of Mr. Kokkinakis violated Article 9 because it was not justified by any "pressing social need."

But the ECHR cannot be relied on to be tough on governments that restrict religious liberty. The court grants to all nations what it calls the "margin of appreciation," or broad discretion to settle the case under customary local norms. In addition, the ECHR seems to have a bias against nontraditional religions.

One has to wonder whether the attitudes of the ECHR will affect other decision makers around the world when they are called upon to decide on religious issues that push the envelope. The judges on the ECHR all come from nations within the European Union. They undoubtedly grew up in the traditionally religious nations of their continent. Are they psychologically biased against new religions, which to them may seem strange or even bizarre?

It seems that governments almost always seek their own short-term goals and try to silence or even persecute any religion that gives them opposition. Governments by nature, if you will, suffer no opposition lightly. The new international guarantees of the freedom of religion are designed to level the playing field and give religious convictions a new, internationally recognized place in the governance of the world. Religious organizations are guaranteed tolerance, acceptance, and a degree of equality with governments. People of faith are granted leave to criticize the state, dissent from it in certain ways, and go to court to vindicate their positions.

But the positions of religious organizations and governments can never be truly equal. Religions and churches have no armies and no power to tax. They are not governments, and, like everyone else, they are subject to the will of governments. It seems that to struggle against governments is an inherent role for churches. Consequently, international law has an overwhelmingly difficult task in attempting to confer on religious bodies the moral and legal capacity to demand and obtain recognition and respect from governments. Governments are being asked to respect spiritual duties that may, as they see it, be adverse to their own interests.

But asserting and vindicating the rights of religious groups need not involve a struggle between known parties and specific differences. Governments often wage war against religion not by strife but by silence. Many governments have constitutions and laws that are ambiguous or silent about religion. In some circumstances, the churches, synagogues, and mosques conclude that the silence that greets them when they are acquiescent may be better than the hostility that would greet them if they were active and articulate.

Much history and many situations today remind people of faith that they should not be too militant in their demands. For example, history will someday outline the struggles of the churches in Eastern and Central Europe to regain their property and their status after the Communists lost control in 1990. Many of the postcommunist regimes, such as those in Lithuania and Slovenia, were headed by former Communists who had never known the Catholic Church. As the churches have struggled to have their property returned, many of the newly secularized governments have resisted. Someday we will know to what extent the new claim to religious freedom now embodied in international law was a factor in the monumental struggles that occurred in postcommunist Europe.

But it is unrealistic and even romantic to think that someday the world will be free of clashes based on religion. On February 27, 2002, a Muslim mob in India stoned a railroad car filled with activists going to the World Hindu Council; the mob then set the train on fire, killing fifty-nine people, mostly women and children. The following day, tens of thousands of Hindus rampaged through Islamic enclaves, burning alive 124 Muslims. In Gujarat, India, the carnage turned 100,000 Muslims into refugees and damaged 20,000 homes and 360 Muslim places of worship. It could be noted that the Hindu-Muslim rivalry is ethnic as well as religious, but the furies in India in 2002 demonstrate vividly that religiously motivated enmity remains a combustible force of tragic dimensions.

Governments have been the enemies of religion for long periods of history. Political leaders do not like anything that calls their broad authority into question. In the past, the governments of China and Japan expelled or executed foreign missionaries, fearing that they would upset the local populace with their message. It may be that governments, even elected leaders, can often be expected to curb the influence of religions. These leaders realize that religious leaders in the past have abused their authority and taken revolutionary positions that would now be considered indefensible. The churches' new reverence for human rights may also surprise and worry government leaders—especially those who are not elected. Churches that are strong advocates of human rights are likely to challenge governments that fail to grant those rights to their citizens, as is now required of every member of the United Nations.

Are there combined moral and political principles that

can bring about an armistice between governments and religions? The best such synthesis to date is the 1981 United Nations Declaration on Religious Freedom. The international community may yet urge its clarification and elevation to a binding covenant. The family of nations is embarrassed by the strictly religious conflicts around the world and believes generally in the rule of law, the fruitfulness of active dialogue, and the use of the powers of conciliation inherent in all religions.

Human rights have become the center of a new global moral language. Religious organizations of all kinds have endorsed the aspirations embodied in the ever-growing collection of UN documents and decisions that embrace and enhance human rights. Can governments come to see religious bodies as friends rather than enemies? If so, there may be a lessening or even termination of governments' centuries-old suspicions that citizens with faith tend to be "subversive."

Governments are created to bring justice and peace to their citizens and to assist other nations in the world community. The number of free countries has slightly increased in recent years, but in 2002, according to the annual ratings of Freedom House, eighty-five countries were free, fifty-nine were partially free, and forty-eight were not free. It can be assumed that in nations that are not free or only partially free, religious freedom is compromised or denied. In the modern world economy, however, governments need to project an image that will attract investors and tourists and foster a good reputation. This is one of the more powerful inducements for all nations to carry out their pledge to the United Nations to promote religious freedom.

Theoretically, the future for religious freedom is bright. Since 1970 more than 30 new democracies have been born around the world and more than 150 major new national, regional, and international instruments on religious freedom have been established. Many are replete with generous commitments to religious pluralism and nondiscrimination.

This amazing moral and religious development has brought a new war for souls. But there has been a reaction in Eastern Europe, sub-Saharan Africa, and Latin America. Nations in these areas are not exactly rejecting the apostles of faith, but they are concerned about all the baggage that such proselytizing brings with it. What the ultimate outcome will be is by no means clear at this time, but it is clear that foreign religious groups should exercise restraint and avoid, in the expression of Vatican II, the shadow of coercion.

All of these developments and the uncertainty of the place of missionaries in various regions have caused theorists and international lawyers to be intentionally ambiguous in defining the guarantees of the 1981 United Nations Declaration on Religious Freedom.

Is this a time when it can be anticipated that governments will be more receptive to religious forces, at least those that already exist in their countries? Perhaps. But some public officials may fear that a coalition of religious forces could forge a lobby in favor of certain judicial norms in respect to divorce, pornography, graft, abortion, and similar topics with religious significance. Governments, as usual, do not want churches to set the agenda. As a result, many governments will seek to inhibit or even silence religious groups that they believe could embarrass political officials by advocating a strict moral code. Churches, for their part, have to recognize that their persuasive power in Europe and elsewhere has been so diminished that they cannot expect to change the moral code of once-Christian nations through decree. Ultimately, it seems fair to say that the governments and churches in the West are not likely to clash openly, because both know that they do not have the political power to prevail.

At this impasse, is it possible that evangelical or fundamentalist Christians will seek to refashion the public morality of the nations where they reside? The answer has to be yes. Such a moment began in the United States just before 1980, when the Moral Majority and the Christian Coalition undertook militant political measures to achieve their objectives. Most of these efforts failed.

International law has tried to maximize the religious freedom of individuals by setting forth principles of conduct for believers, nonbelievers, and governments. The rules and guidelines are generally agreeable to and accepted by all the parties. But by the very nature of the topic, there will always be tensions, conflicts, and even open hostilities among these three groups. There has never been an international legal mechanism that could hammer out resolutions for all of these groups' inherently adversarial positions. However, we may hope that the coming international scrutiny of human rights will help to persuade governments that they must be supportive and even encouraging of all persons of faith and of their communities.

X

The People's Republic of China
and Religious Freedom

I t may not be helpful to say that one particular country
has the worst record on religious freedom in the world. If
we undertook to assign that label, however, and possibly
overlooked Sudan, the People's Republic of China would
have an almost unchallenged claim to that distinction. Year after year the U.S. State Department's Report on Human Rights
declares China's unremitting hostility to Christians and other
religious groups.

It is distressing that China so openly rejects the right to
the free exercise of religion, so clearly a part of customary international law. That vast nation, with some 20 percent of the
human race, was one of the founders of the United Nations—
indeed, it is one of the five permanent members of the Security Council. In 1948 China endorsed the Universal Declaration of Human Rights and in 1999 it ratified the Convention
on Civil and Political Rights. China has become a member of
the World Trade Organization and has made commitments to
abide by all of the rights required by that organization. China
was present in Vienna in 1993 at the World Conference on

Human Rights, and, like 171 other nations, agreed to the final declaration issued by that conference.

Is there some way to explain why China, having joined the world community in so many ways, persists in attitudes and actions toward religion that can be described only as hostile and in violation of the basic commitments of the human race that no religion should be harassed or suppressed? Perhaps.

China has historically been xenophobic, and it has isolated itself in almost every conceivable way. If the government has not been unfavorable to Buddhism, the reason is that this ancient religion does not pose any real challenge to the state. Both before and after its collapse into communism in 1949, China has trampled on any culture or religion that could pose a threat to the ruling powers.

The fascinating story of how such Jesuits as Father Matteo Ricci (1552–1610) brought Western learning and European religion to China demonstrates that China is consistent in its failure to welcome outside ideas. Although this generalization is probably not totally reconcilable with China's embrace of communism in 1949, one must remember that this cultural revolution was achieved by the Long March and the worldwide attraction of Karl Marx's economic theory at that time.

The fear, indeed the paranoia, shown by China toward Christianity and any other religion that threatens Chinese autonomy is not likely to abate as long as the present government or its ideological successor is in power. But the global drive for faith and religious freedom may someday bring a surge in religious feeling in China that could dramatically increase the number of Chinese people of faith. Christians in China and around the world would welcome such a development, but many are aware that if they criticize and berate China, the government in Beijing could become more adamant in its repression of religion.

It is pleasant to imagine that China may be on the brink of accepting more of the human rights and moral values of the West, but all of history suggests otherwise. One does not have to believe in the "clash of civilizations" posited by Samuel Huntington to know that China feels beleaguered, surrounded by forces that would change it in very fundamental ways.

The 2001 State Department Report on Human Rights in China points out bluntly the many ways in which China violates international norms regulating religious freedoms. These reports on China began in 1977 pursuant to a mandate of Congress. As one who has followed these reports year after year, I can state that the information they contain is complete and comprehensive. The diplomats in the U.S. embassy in Beijing and the professionals in human rights at the State Department have coordinated their remarks with the experts at Amnesty International, Human Rights Watch, and the Lawyers Committee on Human Rights. The unfavorable claims about human rights in China that are made in the State Department reports can be believed.

The constitution of the People's Republic of China provides for freedom of religion and freedom not to believe; but, with amazing persistence, the government restricts religious practices to government-sanctioned organizations at registered places of worship. There are five officially recognized religions in China: Buddhism, Taoism, Islam, Protestantism, and Catholicism. A government official supervises the activities of each of these religions. But despite state supervision, the U.S. State Department report asserts that "membership in religions is growing rapidly" (865). Although China's legal code makes it a crime punishable by up to two years in prison for a government official to deprive any citizen of religious freedom, no one is known to have been apprehended under that statute.

The State Department report is as nonjudgmental as a Western product can be when it describes the systematic repression of religious activities, or at least of those religious activities that are perceived to be obstacles to the continuation of an unelected government whose first instinct is self-preservation. The law yearbook of China as quoted in the State Department report reveals that the number of persons arrested for "disturbing the social order" increased from 76,500 in 1998 to 90,000 in 1999. Most experts agree that the increase was due primarily to religious disputes over Falun Gong, evangelical Christian groups, localized Buddhist entities, and the underground or unofficial Catholic Church.

China is one of only a handful of nations that do not have normal diplomatic relations with the Vatican. The Chinese government was openly annoyed when the Vatican canonized 120 Chinese martyrs in 2000 on October 4—Chinese National Day.

Chinese regulations enacted in 1994 and expanded in 2000 include a ban on proselytizing by foreigners. Restrictions on Muslim teaching continue to be tight in China, although the government in part subsidized a pilgrimage to Mecca made by 2,000 Chinese Muslims. The foreign Jewish community in Beijing has held weekly services since 1995, and the Shanghai Jewish community was allowed to hold services in historic Shanghai Synagogue. Mormons meet regularly, but membership in that community is strictly limited to expatriates. Although government officials in Beijing instruct all schools to teach atheism and prohibit the participation of minors in religious education, they have taken little action to bar large numbers of young persons from attending religious services.

The harshest treatment of any religious group in China in 1999 was extended to the Falun Gong. The persons designated by the government as the "core leadership" of this movement were detained and some incarcerated for "endangering state security." According to sources in the Falun Gong, hundreds of its practitioners have been confined to mental hospitals.

Of all of the clashes that Beijing has had with religious groups, the actions taken against the Falun Gong have hurt China's government the most in Western public opinion. It is not clear exactly what this cult (if it is a cult) holds as its basic doctrine, but its attempted elimination (the word is not too strong) is related to the government's general crackdown on other groups deemed to be cults. This policy was incorporated in the October 1999 decision to ban cults under Article 300 of China's criminal law.

Jubilee Campaign, a British human rights group, reported in the London *Times* on February 11, 2000, that secret documents from China revealed that the Beijing government had ordered a ban on a variety of "cults," defining that term to mean any group that refused to register with the government. Sun Jian Xian, a leading Chinese security official, is reported to have told his officers to intensify the crackdown on "hostile Western powers" so that they would not continue their strategies of "Westernizing our country."

On February 17, 2002, Freedom House's Center for Religious Freedom published several secret documents detailing the repression of unregistered Christian churches in China. Also in February 2002, the international Christian community stated that as many of 23,686 Christians had been arrested since 1983, 121 of whom had been killed. On February 2, 2002, the Vatican-based agency FIDES announced that the arrest of Catholics had continued since China had joined the World Trade Organization.

The State Department's report was corroborated on May 2, 2002, by the Third Annual Report of the U.S. Commission on International Religious Freedom. The report warns that the United States should not relax the promotion of religious freedom for the sake of gaining allies in the war on terrorism. The document reprimands China for its violation of religious freedom and suggests that U.S. corporations doing business in China do more to persuade that nation to guarantee religious freedom.

President George W. Bush, visiting China, said on February 2, 2002, that people in China "should be free to choose how they live, how they worship and how they work." Bush's remarks were censored in part by the New China News Agency. The opinions of the West on the state of religious freedom in China are uniformly negative.

It is impossible to predict whether religious freedom will be more acceptable in the near future than it has been in the past. Under a relatively recent law, all of China's approximately 1 million villages are expected to hold competitive elections for village committees. A 1998 revision of the law called for more transparency in the administration of the law, promoting democracy at the grass roots. And the world is watching. The Hong Kong–based Information Center for Human Rights and Democracy and the New York–based organization Human Rights in China, assisted by dissidents, send out voluminous information, which seems more and more frequently to appear in the mainstream press.

The customs that developed over the centuries when China was almost unknown to the Western world cannot be transformed in a short time. If there were a United Nations covenant on religious freedom similar to the 1981 UN Declaration on Religious Freedom, would it have a significant impact on China? No one can be certain. But if the United Nations maintained a listening post in Geneva, New York, or elsewhere to monitor China's compliance with its obligations under the UN Covenant on Religious Freedom, there would at least be one more area where the world could learn about China's egregious stifling of religious voices and practices amid its vast population.

But even the pressures generated by such an international forum would not be able to resolve the tormenting questions of the nature and future of the widely acclaimed right to religious freedom. The questions raised are difficult: Is a nation required to allow missionaries within its territory on the same basis as industrialists, scientists, and professors? Can evangelists claim that they have a right guaranteed by world law to teach their religion comparable to journalists' right to freedom of the press under Article 19 of the Universal Declaration of Human Rights? Should a nation such as China be required to recognize the rights of religious believers to send information about their faith to the Chinese people via the Internet or other comparable means? Is it, in other words, a violation of international law to jam, as Beijing does, the signals of the Voice of America, CNN, and comparable forums for communicating information? Under the new international order that has existed since the several UN covenants on human rights went into effect, are there activities that no nation can refuse to allow—subject, of course, to some reasonable restrictions? And if the Declaration on Religious Freedom became a binding treaty, would each member of the United Nations be required to recognize the right to religious freedom as coequal with the other rights that have become, or are in the process of becoming, customary international law?

These questions are not unreasonable, because China has signed the International Covenant on Economic, Social, and Cultural Rights (ICESCR) and has signed and ratified the Covenant against Torture, the Covenant on the Elimination of Discrimination against Women (CEDAW), and the Covenant on the Rights of the Child (CRC). China is also an active member of the UN Commission on Human Rights. In interesting juxtaposition, the United States has not ratified the ICESCR, the CEDAW, or the CRC. It is clear that China's approach to human rights has developed from the Marxist-Leninist roots of the Chinese Communist party toward a position that gives, at least on paper, some recognition to the universality of human rights. But a different message can be taken from the public record of China's actions, including the violent response to the Tiananmen Square demonstrations and all the other denials of China's obligations under the treaties it has signed and ratified.

An excellent book that summarizes China's struggle with human rights is Rosemary Foot's *Rights beyond Borders: The Global Community and the Struggle over Human Rights in China.* In summarizing the major controversies over human rights in China in recent years, Foot pinpoints the major neuralgic points and apparent contradictions in China's policies. China is ever more conscious of its appearance on the world stage, but it is nevertheless bound to its past practices by the secrecy of its government, its fear of outsiders, and a millennium without elections. Some observers may see Foot as more optimistic than the facts warrant. However, she supports her position by chronicling all the relevant facts about China's struggle to cope with the onslaught of criticism from the United Nations Commission on Human Rights, from NGOs and government entities, and, most important, from public opinion.

In the oceans of ink that have been devoted to chronicling the human rights situation in China, one finds occasional discussions of China's efforts to restrict the number of children in each family and to require women to have abortions in order to achieve a stable birth rate. The moral ramifications of these policies speak for themselves. But the overarching criticism of China from innumerable sources relates to that nation's adherence to traditions and customs of the past that are now being swept into the dustbin of history by the worldwide enthusiasm for those universally accepted human rights which China, almost alone among major nations, is resisting.

People who favor the development of the right to religious freedom lament that China is so fearful of anything that is foreign, new, or "Western." How rapidly China will become "modern" and take its place among the great developed powers of the world is not clear. Those who see the centuries of Chinese culture still reflected in the nation's policies want to be respectful of that venerable heritage. At the same time, people of faith sincerely believe that religion is good for a nation and for its people. Religion can bring values to citizens and help a nation to be peaceful in its relations with other countries. Religion can be a force for peace on a planet where nations are closer than ever before.

People who are not religious and who understandably do not want governments to support religious bodies are often surprised that persons of faith and religious organizations seem to be looking to the government, however subtly, for some support for their position. Christian groups have been following that practice since the time of Constantine. But the United Nations Declaration on the Freedom of Religion (see Appendix A) does not require any favoritism by any government. The declaration simply requires that the state forbid persecution and discrimination; it does not demand that China recognize any religious group or give any church, synagogue, or mosque any preferential treatment not given to any other private entity.

The United Nations Declaration on Religious Freedom does, however, give a religious group a standing different from that of any other entity, such as a club of sports fans or bridge players. Religious groups are entitled by international law to be unencumbered by government bans unless the government has some rational reason to issue them. But religious groups are entitled to more than the right of association and assembly. They are presumed to have been created by individuals in accord with the dictates of their conscience. Therefore, they have rights that are different from—and some would say superior to—the rights of other groups that claim the right to freedom of speech or of the press, the right to assemble, or the right to have their grievances heard by the government.

By signing the International Covenant on Civil and Political Rights, China has agreed to respect and guarantee the political rights—including freedom of religion—recognized in that document. When China reports to the United Nations Human Rights Committee, which monitors compliance with the International Covenant on Civil and Political Rights, it will be challenged and probably rebuked for its failure to live up to its commitment to religious freedom. If the UN Declaration on the Freedom of Religion were upgraded to a covenant and China were required to report on the state of religious freedom in its vast territory, would protections increase for persons of faith? The answer must be yes, at least over the long term.

In all of the lobbying and maneuvering to increase attention to religious freedom, do religious bodies appear to be asking for preferential treatment? Some observers—perhaps many—will think so. But it can be argued that those who want more protection for religious freedom are simply asking for the state to prevent harassment and even persecution for something unique. Many national and international entities related to religion acknowledge, at least silently, that vast numbers of people feel deeply that God has spoken to them and guided them into a particular religion. They believe that it would be sinful to go against what God is guiding or even compelling them to do. For some, disobedience could or would result in eternal damnation.

This is the clear understanding behind the protected status of religious freedom in national and international law. It may not be spelled out, but the sensitivity of individual conscience is the major reason for the protection of religious freedom in the Universal Declaration of Human Rights, the European Convention, the Inter-American Covenant, and especially the UN Declaration on Religious Freedom. The right is, of course, recognized in the First Amendment to the U.S. Constitution, where sixteen words say it well: "Congress shall make no law respecting an establishment of religion, or prohibiting the free exercise thereof. . . ."

The enigmatic unelected leaders of the Communist government in Beijing are being pressed by world opinion to relax their rigid restrictions and grant religious freedom to the millions who might seize it if they had the opportunity. Those officials are fearful. Most or all of them have accepted Marx's thesis that religion is the "opium of the masses," but they also understand that a feeling is increasing in the world that there should be a place of sanctuary for persons who sincerely and profoundly feel that God, their conscience, or some mysterious but powerful source is requiring them to do what the government forbids. Therefore, those in charge of the government in Beijing will continue to negate the validity of the claims of persons who want to be openly religious. They may scorn them as the victims of delusions or as the psychologically feeble who yearn for a crutch. But mostly the rejoinder in Beijing will be that Christianity in any form is a product of the West and is "subversive" of the history and culture of Asia.

I heard this sentiment expressed loudly and clearly in a discussion with eleven high-level officials from Beijing. The State Department asked me to talk about human rights to these visiting dignitaries. It was a tough afternoon. The visitors—all Communists and veterans of the struggle to silence dissidents in the People's Republic—had their speeches ready. Human rights are a construct of the West. Foreign-born Christians have no place in China. As the most populous nation on Earth, China has a right not to be harassed by persons whose values are not Chinese.

Before globalization, attended as it has been by such organizations as CNN and the World Trade Organization, one would feel that the Chinese bureaucrats would be able to prevail for the indefinite future. With the amazing coming together of the world, however, dictatorships may give way to democracies and countless people spiritually starved by the omnipresent secularism and consumerism may turn to some form of religious experience and demand that their governments allow them to seek a spiritual way of life that is now forbidden. Authorities in China may have surmised that the Falun

Gong was a subversive endeavor. This may be why they have tried to crush it. The universally bad press that resulted for China when it took its actions against the Falun Gong may or may not have brought sobering thoughts to China's leaders. But the bad press will only increase, as the future of religious liberty in China is now a deepening concern for religious and nonreligious people everywhere.

Although faith in an unseen god is mysterious and sometimes frightening for everyone, China sees it as a grave threat, an assault from outside the nation and a warning of dangers to come. To Chinese officials, Christians must seem to be a special danger. They believe that they have a clear mandate from Christ to preach the Gospel to the ends of the Earth. They have had successes and failures in China. The French Jesuits operated a prestigious university with law and medical faculties in Shanghai until the Communist government seized it and shut it down. Protestant missionaries from the United States and elsewhere created centers of Christian culture until, once again, China's government suppressed them. Christians and non-Christians alike wonder whether China will ever allow such enterprises in the future. Would Christian missionaries be permitted if they restricted themselves to humanitarian works like Mother Teresa?

If the Beijing government refuses to admit missionaries, will Christian groups who recognize that they cannot obtain visas to do religious work in China create some vehicle of evangelization akin to the Voice of America? With the ever more sophisticated means of communication available, Christians will not remain silent. They will create instrumentalities that China cannot jam. Ironically, the resistance of present-day China to the Gospel will only intensify the determination of Christians to evangelize its people.

During the twentieth century, Catholic and Protestant missionaries went in large numbers to Africa, Asia, and Latin America as part of formal efforts to colonize those regions. That vehicle is no longer available but it was effective for Catholics; the number of Roman Catholics in Africa, for example, increased from 3 million in 1900 to 120 million in the year 2000. As a result of such efforts at evangelization, China undoubtedly connects missionaries with colonialism. For centuries China has resisted the cultural invasion of foreigners; it seems to wish to adhere to that principle, although the invasion of Xerox, DuPont, and Coca-Cola may be irresistible. Many of the factors that promote the spread of such corporations in the global market also aid people of faith in their efforts to cross borders to convert others.

Christians feel obligated to spread their faith, as Christ urged them to do on several occasions. Of course, international law does not want to *impede* Christians in their attempts to evangelize, but to what extent is international law required to *facilitate* the teaching of Christianity? The question confronts the leaders of every nation. Christianity by its very nature seeks to radiate its convictions, and even if it cannot call for special treatment, it nevertheless is entitled at least to the right of free speech granted to secular organizations.

At the same time, Christians have to be humble about their mistakes of the past. As they claim liberty to preach their faith, Christians must recognize that their offenses against the free exercise of religion include the actions taken by Torquemada as the grand inquisitor, the torturer of Jews, Moors, and other "heretics."

Those inside and outside of China who are asking for religious freedom appeal to the 1981 United Nations Declaration on the Elimination of All Forms of Intolerance and of Discrim-

ination Based on Religion or Belief. In Article 1(3), that declaration asserts that "freedom to manifest one's religion or belief
may be subject only to such limitations as are prescribed by
law and are necessary to protect public safety, order, health or
morals or the fundamental rights and freedoms of others."
Persons who claim religious freedom in China also rely on that
nation's duty under Article 4(2) of the declaration to "make all
efforts to enact or rescind legislation where necessary to prohibit any such discrimination, and to take all appropriate measures to combat intolerance on the grounds of religion."

Every nation must make accommodations to religion
as required by the new international law of human rights.
China appears to be more resistant to the required accommodation than other countries. But some religious groups can be
overly assertive of their claims. For example, certain individuals wanted to go so far as to prevent China from entering the
World Trade Organization until Beijing gave more respect to
all human rights, especially religious freedom. Others reasoned
that bringing China into the noncommunist and pluralistic
world of the World Trade Organization would induce that nation to be more respectful of human rights.

The clash between organized religion and the adamantly
antireligious policies of Beijing may not be resolved for some
time. If Beijing departs from its Communist basis as Moscow
did, there may be some easing of the war against religion on
the part of Chinese leaders. What is needed is not necessarily
some great awakening in the hearts of China's rulers but the
coming of a broad and deep understanding that any defiance
by any government of reasonable religious practices violates
basic decency as well as the law of human rights that has developed since World War II. A new era is here. For centuries
governments were able to deny religious bodies their appro-

priate rights, and religious groups were able to use secular governments to achieve their sacred obligations—but no longer. Coercion by either governments or religious bodies is impermissible. The Second Vatican Council in its 1965 decree on religious freedom emphatically clarified the new principle in a statement that China would do well to heed: "A wrong is done when government imposes on its people, by force or fear or other means, the repression or repudiation of any religion."

XI

Religious Freedom and the Muslim World

As one looks at the vast literature and the arcane controversies about the past and present teachings of Islam, one has to wonder if any worldwide juridical authority could define and apply international principles of religious freedom to the Muslim world; or, more pointedly, if the rulings of such a tribunal could ever win acceptance in the world of Islam—some fifty nations and 1.2 billion adherents.

One of several complicating factors is the virtual inseparability of Islam and the culture that is both its cause and its effect. The Shari'a, or Islamic code of law, is derived not merely from the Koran but also from centuries of debate and discussions by men (never by women) who, sometimes influenced by political and cultural situations, made rulings that may have looked to the Koran and Shari'a for advancement of their own positions.

Even a cursory inspection of Islamic history reveals that there is no central authority to speak on behalf of Islam, and the various teachings of the several periods of that history do not necessarily cohere. Indeed, it is difficult not to be overwhelmed by the complexity and contradictions of Islamic theology.

Furthermore, some Islamic nations have reserved the right not to be controlled by international law. When some Muslim countries ratified the international covenants on human rights, they stated express exceptions to the effect that their nations' compliance is subject to the dictates of Shari'a, similar to the United States' reservations that its commitments under such covenants are subject to the requirements of the U.S. Constitution. Under such reservations, international obligations under the covenants are rendered invalid if they contradict the essential teachings of the bodies of law in question.

Of course, several European nations have criticized certain reservations asserted by the United States, such as its insistence that in ratifying the Universal Covenant against Torture it was not making any commitment to which it was not already bound by the Eighth Amendment's ban on "cruel and unusual punishment." It can indeed be argued that such conduct by the United States is reprehensible. But the broader reservations made by Islamic nations to the effect that they will not yield to any obligation not allowed by the Shari'a appear to be a clear undercutting of the very purpose of the treaty, and thus are impermissible under the provisions of the Vienna Treaty on Treaties.

As it currently stands, any proposed covenant on religious freedom would face that formidable barrier in the Islamic world. Many Islamic nations have already asserted flatly and repeatedly that they will not yield to any norm of religious freedom that violates what they perceive to be an obligation derived from the teachings of the Prophet.

Most people would agree that a nation has the right to resist international norms that go directly against a fundamental aspect of a national religion. But does this mean that a small group, or even a large majority, in control of a nation has a right to follow religious practices directly forbidden by global standards that arguably rise to the level of customary international law?

The answer has to be yes. Although most would admit that the supremacy of conviction and conscience cannot always be respected, this is a different question. Any world commission or tribunal charged with denying to a government the right to do what it feels is required by divine command would have an impossibly heavy burden of proof.

If someday a world committee on religious freedom is created, similar to the several UN bodies that monitor compliance with other human rights covenants, would the operating principles of that new group be clear and consistent enough to win the allegiance of the world? Several Islamic nations have already proclaimed that for them the dictates of the Shari'a will always take precedence over contradictory international norms. Some people would argue that the policies of these nations should be accepted because it is the deliberate, conscientious judgment of the individuals in these countries that no outside norm that conflicts with their own solemn covenants, anchored in their conscience, can be followed. Those who advance this argument have a powerful case. Most would shudder at the thought of an international body, however impartial and respected, claiming that it trumps conclusions based on religious faith made by sincere adherents.

But difficult questions persist. Can international law generate no norms that interfere with the religious freedom of any

believers or nonbelievers? Is international law powerless to decree that such Muslim nations as Indonesia and Saudi Arabia
have an obligation to tolerate Christians and other missionaries as they evangelize to the citizens of those nations? In fact, a
strong position exists in the Islamic world that no one has a
right to change his or her religion, and despite the development of the Declaration on Religious Freedom, many Muslim
nations retain the ban. Such a ban is common among religions: Catholics cannot claim any right in Catholic tradition
that allows them to change their religion; the situation for Jews
is the same. Every religion has strong words for those who de-
part: they are defectors, heretics, schismatics, or traitors. They
are often seen as the equivalent of Judas.

Islam shares the reluctance of most religions to accept
the right to change one's religion. Should that long-standing reluctance be denied recognition in international law in the name
of a right to religious freedom that, it must be confessed, is
relatively new in human history? The questions and the dilemmas get more excruciating as one analyzes the need for *some*
global entity to sort out the desire of believers and nonbelievers to alter world law to support their views.

The state of religious freedom in Muslim countries is
possibly the most complicated of all the church–state situations of the 191 nations of the United Nations. Historically and
theologically, the Muslim countries have not been receptive
to other religions. Nevertheless, the situation for Christians in
many Islamic countries is tolerable, perhaps because Christian
groups have never obtained a substantial presence in the Muslim regions of the world.

Of course, some people would simply not press for religious freedom in Islamic nations at all. This path would surely

be a mistake. To concede that religious human rights are not enforceable in some countries would lessen the importance of all human rights in the covenants of the United Nations. Human rights are indivisible and all are of equal worth. This central teaching was reiterated and reinforced in the 1993 Vienna Declaration of Human Rights, agreed to by 172 nations.

When one considers the successful recognition of political rights and observes the constant progress these rights have made over the years, one may wonder whether the right to religious freedom should have been placed in that category. Of course, if the framers of the Universal Declaration of Human Rights and the Covenant on Political Rights understood some of the difficulties that would surface with regard to religious freedom, they might never have named that freedom in their historic documents at all. However, religious freedom is named there, on the same level as every other political right. Will it ever be implemented on the same basis as its coequal political rights?

The thesis of this book has been that religious freedom has been elevated to the status of customary international law, and therefore its observance should be monitored and supervised like other basic rights of a political nature. But the question keeps recurring: Are feelings about religious freedom so volatile that it is unrealistic to hope for even-handed treatment of religious freedom at the international level? Complicating the quest for some form of international protection of religious freedom is the fact that, for now, only a few voices from religious bodies are calling for a supranational review of the rights of persons of faith. Of course, with globalization bringing people and nations together in unprecedented ways, people who care for religious freedom may want to share a platform

with the ever more powerful forces calling for freedom of the
press, freedom of assembly, and freedom to do business beyond and across borders.

As globalization and the World Trade Organization make
international trade and all types of business communications
commonplace, it may no longer be realistic or even possible
to prevent religious communications between the institutions of the Western world and the citizenry of Islamic nations. Churches in the West need not even send missionaries;
they can send their messages by transborder electronic means
that nations cannot keep from their territories any more than
they can stem the intake of omnipresent polluted air or acid
rain. That nations are increasingly powerless to exclude such
unwanted influences is simply a sign of the times and seemingly will only increase in the future.

In a sense, intolerance is taught not by religion but by political leaders who use religion for their own purposes. Buddhism does not set forth any particular beliefs or rituals that it
seeks to impose. Hinduism has always acknowledged different
means to obtain spiritual liberties. Christians have come to see
elements of the one God expressed in other religions. Muslims
adhere to the mandates of the Koran, and that sacred text urges
them to respect diversity in religion. The Koran (2:256) states
flatly: "There must be no coercion in matters of faith." It adds
(109:6) that people of different religions must be allowed to go
their own ways: "unto you, your moral law, and unto me, mine."

To survey how Islam actually operates in the Muslim
world is a daunting task. The essays in Kevin Boyle and Juliet
Sheen's *Freedom of Religion and Belief* make it clear that international standards do not require the separation of church or
religion from the state. Indeed, a large number of countries—
indeed, possibly the majority—require a relationship between

the political community and historically dominant religions. Boyle and Sheen conclude that there is a consensus among specialists in human rights that "religion and belief should be the subject of a new international rights convention." But they do not regard the formation of such a convention to be an immediate objective.

The two-volume study *Religious Human Rights in Global Perspective,* published in 1996 by the Law and Religion Program at Emory University, makes a magnificent contribution to the deepening understanding of how religious freedom in all its dimensions can be protected by international law. But even this comprehensive work cannot speak definitively on how traditional Islam can be reconciled with the advance of religious freedom.

Despite the Koran's endorsement of tolerance, the universal Islamic Declaration of Human Rights of 1981 makes it clear that it recognizes no distinction between law and religion. Abdullahi An-Na'im, a noted authority, wrote in the *Human Rights Quarterly* in 1987, "It would be heretical for a Muslim who believes that Shari'a is the final and ultimate foundation of the law of God to maintain that any aspect of the law is open to revision and reformulation by mere mortal and fallible human beings. To do so is to allow human beings to correct what God has decreed."

The sovereignty of Allah is recognized in the constitutions of several Muslim nations. It is also common for Muslim states to proclaim Islam to be their official religion; Pakistan, Afghanistan, Algeria, Bangladesh, Egypt, Jordan, Malaysia, and Morocco have done so. Four that have not are Libya, Turkey, Syria, and Sudan.

The constitutions of most Muslim states have expressly upheld the principle of religious freedom and have banned

discrimination on the basis of religion. But most of these constitutions contain the caveat that the exercise of religious freedom is subject to considerations of public order, health, and/or
morals. Further, many Islamic countries expressly require the
head of state to be a Muslim. In such nations, missionary work
to convert Muslims to any other faith is usually restricted, but
efforts to convert non-Muslims to Islam are encouraged.

In countries that embark on such programs of systematic
Islamization, several forms of discrimination against religious
minorities are evident, but some voices in the Islamic world
have opposed such discrimination. In 1987 the Arab Organization for Human Rights criticized governments that used the
Shari'a to support their "one-sided and self-serving interpretation of the Islam doctrine." In his useful book *Faith* and *Human Rights,* Robert Traer has assembled an assortment of such
material relating to Muslim defenders of human rights.

In Islamic nations, conflicts between the vindication of
Muslim ideas and the concept of religious freedom are often
resolved in favor of the former. In May 2002, for example,
Saudi Arabia deported two Filipino Christians who had been
found to be in possession of a Bible and some Christian CDs.
The Christians had violated the Saudi Arabian law forbidding
the public expression of any religious belief other than Islam.

Any international monitoring of the state of religious
freedom in Islamic nations would have to be detailed and comprehensive. But could international assessment of the situation in the Muslim world lead to productive outcomes? If
there were a UN committee to monitor compliance with international standards, would its activities bring about a broader
religious tolerance in Islamic countries? No one really knows,
but if there were such a forum, dissidents such as the two Fil-
ipinos expelled from Saudi Arabia in 2002—and thousands of
others—would have a place to go to register their complaints.

It would be at least a small step in an effort to guarantee that the religious freedom that is so clearly mandated by international law would have a place where it could be vindicated.

Of course, any future evaluation of the state of religious freedom in the Islamic world has been enormously complicated by the attack on the United States on September 11, 2001, by nineteen Muslim hijackers from several Islamic countries. Their mandate and their message may never be completely discovered, but the undeniable meaning of the event to most observers is that certain factions in the Islamic world have an intense animosity toward certain elements of U.S. life, including perhaps the way Christianity is presented or practiced.

Any hope of a rapprochement between the United States and Muslim countries has been shattered, or at least delayed. Suspicions about the Muslim community in the United States have multiplied and will not easily be eliminated. It is clear that the Muslim terrorists who changed the world on September 11, 2001, might not have operated on any theological convictions derived from Islam, but their recklessness will long be connected somehow with the teaching of the prophet Muhammad.

Built into the idea that religion and government should be rather rigidly separated is the feeling that religious people will use the power of government for their own selfish objectives if they can. There is a related belief that political figures will manipulate religious bodies to support similarly ignoble secular objectives if they can. The terrorism of September 11, 2001, is destined to deepen in millions of minds the knowledge that religion can spawn dreams, delusions, and dangers, and the preexisting apprehensions about the interplay of government and religion may well increase.

It is possible that the U.S. public will, after suffering the September 11 attacks, learn a great deal about Islam. Of course, even if Americans do become acquainted with the long and turbulent history of that religion, they may not feel that they have a reliable grasp on what the Islamic tradition really holds with respect to religious freedom. These new and profound anxieties about the ways in which Islamic nations interpret the Muslim religion may prompt Americans to desire the creation of a United Nations covenant on religious freedom and the establishment of a United Nations committee to monitor the state of religious freedom. That such a positive result might grow from the horrors of September 11 would be ironic and wonderful indeed.

XII

The World's Jewish Community and Religious Freedom

I t would be unthinkable to consider the right to religious freedom without reflecting on the perennial denial of that right to the Jewish people. We may hope that the surge in the defense of international human rights ongoing since the creation of the United Nations will usher in an age that finally brings some religious liberty to the Jewish people. This would only be just, as it is self-evident that the birth of the international recognition of human rights is due in important ways to the 6 million who died in the Holocaust.

The Holocaust and Jewish Religious Freedom

In a real sense, the world's attempt to develop international protections for religious freedoms has been prompted and made necessary by what has been inflicted on the Jewish people throughout history. It was the Holocaust more than any other event that brought about the international efforts to protect and promote human rights: the murder of 6 million Jews led directly to the international recognition of the crime of genocide and the comparable offense of crimes against humanity.

The world felt such guilt after the Holocaust that it began initiatives designed to prevent anything like it from ever happening again. Notwithstanding this ideal, it must be remembered that over the course of the twentieth century, up to 100 million people perished in the labor camps of the Soviet Union, in the Cultural Revolution in China, and in the infernos of the Balkans, Rwanda, Cambodia, and other centers of horror.

It is almost impossible to stop thinking about the Holocaust. After a two-hour tour of the Holocaust museum in Washington, D.C., one is unable to speak. How could all this have happened? Can it really be true that the United States could have or should have known about the Holocaust while it was happening, yet did not do all that it could? Books, revelations, memoirs keep appearing. The words and stories of Elie Wiesel are more haunting all the time, while the silence and the guilt of Christians become more unbearable as the years go on.

Nor did the persecution of the Jews end with the close of World War II. The most severe denial of religious freedom to Jews after the Holocaust may have been the repression of Jews in the USSR, which led to an exodus of some million Jews. These emigrants, largely to the United States and Israel, felt compelled to give up their privileges and professions in the USSR in order to travel to foreign nations where they would be able to practice their faith. The United Nations and the world community had no moral or legal machinery capable of forcing the Kremlin to live up to its obligations to guarantee religious freedom. As a result, through the power of U.S. law, the United States made a place for these Jews who felt that their conscientious desire to practice their faith required them to leave a land inhabited by their forebears for many generations.

The Jews have suffered other repercussions in many other nations since the Holocaust, yet still the United Nations has never moved to develop a genuine enforceable covenant to guarantee the rights it recognizes. A question arises about the possible presence of invisible but real anti-Semitism.

Modern Anti-Semitism and Jewish Religious Freedom

The long, tragic story of the persecution of the Jewish people needs to be told and retold. Otherwise, people might forget— or might come to want to forget. But this is a story that has no words of regret and lament to match its anguish, and the specter of anti-Semitism continues to haunt the world. How can a world aware of human rights as never before allow anti-Semitism to persist and even to grow?

The rise of anti-Semitism in Europe in 2002 was alarming. Although none can definitively pinpoint which of several happenings was most responsible for the trend, one fundamental cause seems to be the prejudice of some members of the Islamic world against Israel.

A pervasive countermovement, however, has developed in countries reluctant to do anything that would encourage or enhance the ability of Muslim nations to express anti-Semitic views. If one looks at the history of Western culture, it seems fair to say that Christian nations have spread anti-Semitism in ways that almost everyone now laments. Today the anti-Semitic attitudes and observations of the Muslim nations and to some extent the Christian nations deepen a sincere conviction of many persons, both religious and nonreligious, that society should be neutral in respect to religions. At the very least, many feel that national actors should be inhibited from articulating views that are clearly not in favor of pluralism.

When one considers the persistence of anti-Semitism, the question keeps recurring: Would a world authority charged with protecting religious liberty have a salutary effect on efforts to curb global anti-Semitism? The role of law is always limited, and certainly is so in its efforts to combat deep-seated prejudices going back centuries. The efficacy of law is even more questionable when the prejudice it is designed to combat is against a worldwide ancient religion. But laws against hatred can work. At the very least, they can serve as examples, and presumably, over time, they can change attitudes.

The Catholic Church and Jewish Religious Freedom

History suggests that anti-Semitism is a sin that is more persistent and pervasive than the hatred of any other religion. The Christian centuries are so filled with anti-Semitic literature and deeds that it is painful even to recall them, and the Catholic Church is almost certainly the first and greatest offender. This is the message of a searing book, *The Anguish of the Jews*, by the late Father Edward Flannery. The facts of what the Church has done to the Jews through the centuries are almost beyond belief. The ghettos of the Middle Ages, the persecutions of the Inquisition, and the perpetual discrimination against the Jews constitute a legacy for which the Catholic Church and the Second Vatican Council in its statement on the Jewish people express sorrow and regret.

When one argues that religious freedom should be elevated to an enforceable human right guaranteed by a world tribunal, the question arises as to whether this aspiration, in the context of anti-Semitism, can be attained. Reviewing the indefensible way Christian nations have treated the Jewish people, one could conclude that there is something almost inherent in Christianity that promotes anti-Judaism. That concept was implicitly accepted by many Christians for many centuries, and the insidiousness of the idea was made clear when a Christian country, Germany, carried out a mass slaughter of the Jews simply because they were Jews.

As debate continues about the conduct and the culpability of the Catholic Church during World War II, one cannot help wondering whether Catholicism at that time had within it an implicit acceptance of the idea that Christians had a right, or even a duty, to punish the Jews for their lack of faith in Christianity. Although that question makes Christians nervous and embarrassed, they are gradually recognizing that it will not go away. Observers may differ on whether Pope Pius XII did all he could to save Jews from the wrath of Hitler, but no one can deny that the disparagement of the Jews for centuries by the Catholic and Protestant churches set up what Father Flannery called "the contempt of the Jews."

The basic question is whether there is something inherent in Christianity that leads to anti-Semitism. At least since Vatican II, Catholics would like to deny any such flaw, but Catholics expressed "contempt of the Jews" for so many centuries that one has to wonder whether anti-Semitism has entered into the bloodstream of Catholic culture. One could hope that this is not so, but the persistence and pervasiveness of anti-Semitism suggest that even if world law enforced religious freedom with great zeal, prejudices and biases, although unjustified in Christian teaching, might still reside in the mental and emotional attitudes of Catholics.

Catholics are not alone. Protestants probably share the virus of anti-Semitism to the same extent. Muslims can also be intolerant, although the paucity of Jews in the Muslim world may suggest that this prejudice can be traced in part to the hostility that frequently is extended to any small minority in a community and, of course, to the issue of Israel.

Despite all of the attendant difficulties, it is clear that

there is a need for some world entity to define the rights to religious freedom held by Jews in the diaspora and by Jews and non-Jews in the State of Israel. But it is also clear that the decrees of any international tribunal that may be established will have little chance of being accepted or enforced unless the non-Jews of the world clarify and define their positions on the freedoms that the entire Jewish community deserves and requires.

The Second Vatican Council attempted to do just that for the Catholic Church in 1965. Not everyone is entirely satisfied with the results, but for the first time ever the Church repudiated some of its past errors and proclaimed that religious freedom in the fullest sense is owed to Jewish people everywhere. The council's statement declares that "the church . . . rejects any persecution against any man. For this reason and for the sake of common patrimony with the Jews, she decries hatred, persecution, displays of anti-Semitism staged against the Jews at whatever time in history and by whomsoever. She does so, not moved by political reasons, but impelled by the gospel of pure love." The World Council of Churches, which represents most Protestants and some Orthodox bodies, has issued comparable statements.

In its declaration on Jewish-Christian relations the Second Vatican Council lamented the dreadful record of Christians' mistreatment of the Jews through the centuries. The unprecedented statement, promulgated on October 28, 1965, built upon the work of the World Council of Churches, which in 1948 issued this strong statement:

> We call upon all the churches we represent to denounce anti-Semitism, no matter what its origin, as absolutely irreconcilable with the profession and

practice of the Christian faith. Anti-Semitism is a
sin against God and man. Only as we give convinc-
ing evidence to our Jewish neighbors that we seek
for them the common rights and dignities which
God wills for his children can we come to such a
meeting with them as would make it possible to
share with them the best which God has given us in
Christ.

This bold and unprecedented declaration was supple-
mented in 1961 in the World Council's "Resolution on Anti-
Semitism":

The Assembly renews this plea in view of the fact
that situations continue to exist in which Jews are
subject to discrimination and even persecution.
The Assembly urges its member churches to do
all in their power to resist every form of anti-
Semitism. In Christian teaching, the historic events
which led to the Crucifixion should not be so presented as to impose upon the Jewish people of
today responsibilities which must fall on all humanity, and not on one race or community. Jews
were the first to accept Jesus, and Jews are not the
only ones who do not yet recognize him.

Later, in 1975, the World Council of Churches, meeting in
Nairobi, reacted with vehemence against the charge that Zionism was a form of racism.

The Vatican statement, although bold in some ways,
proved in the end to be an inadequate response to the Church's
centuries-long denial of religious freedom to the Jewish com-

munities of Europe. Hearing the statement, the Jewish people, still trying to recover from the death camp at Auschwitz, were understandably skeptical. However, the Vatican declaration, passed in a final vote of 2,221 to 98, is clearly central to the Catholic Church's modern thinking about religious freedom; hence its eight paragraphs are reproduced as Appendix B.

The declaration by the Second Vatican Council, the first document on Catholic-Jewish relations made by an ecumenical council in the history of the Church, does not expressly refer to the Holocaust or to the establishment of Israel. Since these two happenings are central to the modern Jewish psyche, the failure even to mention them left the Jewish community dissatisfied with what they saw and heard in the pronouncement. Later guidelines promulgated by the Holy See in 1975 were also disappointing to not a few observers of the evolution of the Vatican's thinking on Judaism.

However, there have been dramatic developments in the relations between the Catholic Church and the Jewish people. The initiatives of Pope John Paul II to improve Catholic-Jewish relations have been unique in the history of the Church; for example, he has extended diplomatic recognition to Israel and has visited that country. Rabbi James Rudin, a prominent spokesman for the Jewish community in the United States, has said more than once that Pope John Paul II has done more to develop harmonious Catholic-Jewish relations than any previous pope.

In 1992 the Catholic Church issued a new universal catechism that incorporates the progressive steps that have been taken in the Church's teaching related to Jews and Judaism. The catechism rejects the existence of collective Jewish guilt for the death of Jesus, recalls the Jewish roots of Christianity, and again condemns genocide, persecution, and discrimination "by race or religion." The catechism incorporates Pope

John Paul II's teaching that the covenant between God and the Jews has not been broken and retains its validity.

Nevertheless, some friends of Israel sense the ambiguity with which some Christians view the State of Israel. For centuries Christians believed that the dispersion of the Jewish people was a divinely ordained punishment for orchestrating the crucifixion. That idea, never defensible by appeals to history or theology, has now all but passed out of the minds of Christians. But until it disappears completely, Christians will not be truly prepared to extend to the Jewish community the fullness of freedom that has been bestowed on others by the Universal Declaration of Human Rights and the UN covenants on human rights or to guarantee to Jews all the other privileges that should now be available to every national and ethnic group in the world.

The long history of discrimination against the Jews places them in a special category in the struggle to obtain some level of global legal protection for the practice of religion. The Jewish community has the first claim to such protection, because it has been victimized and denied its right to religious freedom more often and more persistently than any other religious minority. Indeed, it seems safe to say that if the world cannot extend religious freedom to the Jews, who have been denied religious liberty so often, there is doubt as to whether the world can really be expected to give adequate protection to other religions. The recent developments in the Catholic Church's approach to the Jewish community testify that finally the Church, for theological and jurisprudential reasons, is recognizing that it has a special obligation to work diligently to secure religious freedom for Jews.

But the brutality of the Holocaust raises the basic question whether a worldwide system of vigilance over the observance of human rights and a juridical system to punish violations of those rights could prevent future Holocausts. Persons of faith may claim that God ordains the persecution of his own people, as he at least seems to permit it. After all, God never promised the Jews or the Christians an easy time. Robert Royal's book *The Catholic Martyrs of the Twentieth Century* chronicles the staggering number of martyrs between 1900 and 2000—in the range of 100 million if one counts those killed by the Communists in the USSR, China, and Cambodia. The number of persons martyred in Latin America alone is enormous. The murders of Christians in Vietnam, Korea, and regions of Africa are also numerous.

The Second Vatican Council seems to have accepted continued martyrdom as inevitable. In *Lumen gentium* the council stated that "to give this highest witness for love to all, paradoxically for one's persecutors, has been the calling of some Christians from earliest times and will always be."

Persons of faith must reflect on this prediction and the centuries of experience behind it. But the human rights revolution rejects any notion of the inevitability of violence against international human rights. The recognition of the offenses of genocide and crimes against humanity established after World War II has created a new universality of morality and law. Everyone is struggling to find an appropriate place for the right to religion in that new scheme of things. That search is likely to be complicated and lengthy, but the awful memory of the Holocaust will not allow the human family to rest until there is certainty that humankind has done everything in its power to guarantee the precious right of every individual in the global village to worship as he or she chooses.

The recognition of the unique status of the Jews in the world has caused grief and guilt in the Christian community in the years since the Holocaust, but could future acts of Christian justice permit that guilt to subside and even vanish? Persons of faith will have to ponder on what God desires and intends. At present Jews and other non-Christians have a right to be skeptical about the permanence of the current Christian sorrow and regret for what the Church has done to the Jews over the centuries. But for now, Christians have repudiated their massive denial of basic human rights to the Jews. Moreover, such a denial can now be seen not only as a fundamental abdication of the Christian faith but also as an abdication of the human rights guaranteed by international law to the Jewish people and to all of God's children.

The State of Israel and Jewish Religious Freedom

The status of religious freedom in modern Israel reflects the contradictions and paradoxes in almost everyone's approach to the contours of religious freedom. Israel's Declaration of Independence specifically states that Israel will be "a Jewish state." Israeli law provides that "the values of the state of Israel as a Jewish and democratic state" are the basis for human rights in Israel. This 1992 law enjoins any group espousing aims or taking actions to negate the existence of Israel as the "state of the Jewish people" from registering as a political party and running for the Knesset. The Jewishness of the State of Israel is further reflected in its law of return, which confers upon every Jew the right to immigrate.

The church-state arrangement in Israel does not fit easily into any single category of religion-state relations. The centrality of Judaism in Israel must be viewed in line with its Declaration of Independence, which states that Israel "will guarantee freedom of religion and conscience, of language, education and culture." Israeli law contains no provisions that confer on

Judaism the status of a state religion. This is noteworthy because the separation between government and religion is as alien to Judaism as it is to Islam.

Israeli law gives special attention to religious feelings. Penalties are imposed on persons who disturb religious exercises or who utter words calculated to outrage the religious feelings or beliefs of persons of faith. Although the Supreme Court of Israel regularly seeks to extend religious freedoms, not a few observers complain that statutory and decisional law gives preference to persons of faith and particularly to Orthodox Jews. The ultimate premise of these objectors is not clear. Do they feel that the Jewish leaders of Israel must rule as if Israel were just another secular state? Are they implying that faithful Jews in Israel, despite or even because of all the discrimination faced by Jews through the centuries, should renounce any special protection or help from the government?

The government of Israel exemplifies in a unique way the dilemmas facing a new nation whose institutions and laws reflect the international human rights that since 1948 have become customary international law. Should Israeli Jews seek to renounce all encouragement, support, and alliance with their government? Should Israel seek to be a dramatic example of a government that neither subsidizes nor discourages any religious group?

Criticism of the support that the Israeli government gives to organized Jewish religious groups can be heard in various places. No doubt, some comes from individuals who criticize Israel for personal reasons. But another critical view of the relationship of government and religion in Israel is held by scholars and activists who sincerely and earnestly think that strict separation is always better for both government and religion. This position has surely not been the dominant view in history or in present-day Israel.

Notwithstanding the short-term resolution of any of these questions, the autonomy granted to the Orthodox Jewish community in Israel will continue to be a matter of controversy in Israel and around the world.

The United Nations and Jewish Religious Freedom

The Jewish community in the United States and around the world has reason to feel that the United Nations and its agencies do not fight anti-Semitism with all the moral and practical means at their disposal. In other words, in its attitude toward the Jewish community, the United Nations has not risen above the nations that created it.

The topic is, of course, complicated by the allegations made by some Palestinians that Zionism is a form of racism. That slogan, first uttered in the United Nations General Assembly in 1975, arose again at the United Nations Conference on Racism in South Africa in 2001. The concept that Zionism is a form of racism is an expression of the anti-Semitism of the world after Hitler. It is based on the assumption that Jews had no right to turn their religion into a political force, but this attempt to delegitimize Zionism is a frontal assault on the religious freedom of the entire worldwide Jewish community. If a United Nations commission or tribunal on religious freedom were in existence, there is no question that it would hold that any religion could assume any political form that its followers felt was required. Jews in the State of Israel are entitled to use the usual processes by which law everywhere decides matters regarding the proper ownership or occupation of property.

The linking of Judaism and Zionism complicates the already difficult issue of anti-Semitism. It is not well known that after World War II most European Jews who survived were almost required to resettle in Israel. Some of them were afraid that if they resettled in Europe, another persecution would come. In addition, many Jews wanted to follow the age-old dream of spiritual and political Zionism—the gathering of the Jews in the land God had promised them.

If there had been a timely settlement of the claims of the Palestinians rather than four wars and a continuing stalemate over the issue, would there now be less anti-Semitism in the world? No one can say, but it is clear that public sentiment against Israel's leaders and sympathy for the Palestinians complicates the question of anti-Semitism and the issue of religious freedom for people of Jewish ancestry.

The Jewish majority in Israel have further complicated the issue of religious freedom under international law by insisting that traditional Jewish law, rather than a secular arrangement enacted by the Knesset, governs the institution of marriage in Israel. When the issue arises of guaranteeing religious liberties by creating an international tribunal for that purpose, the question of the use of ecclesiastical law in Israel always surfaces. The complexity of the bias against Jews cannot be an excuse for rigid laws enshrining the moral attitude of the majority. Such laws show a lack of the caring, concern, and love that all people owe to all fellow human beings. This concern is required by what the United Nations Declaration of Human Rights describes as the spirit of brotherhood.

Could a worldwide system designed to prevent and punish anti-Semitism in all its forms work? That depends on how one interprets the potential and the effectiveness of laws designed to stop conduct based on contempt or disdain for the

equality of other human beings. The theory behind laws or ordinances that establish a separate category of "hate crimes" is
that civil or criminal penalties can sometimes deter the out-
ward manifestations of inner prejudices. The theory is plausible, perhaps even unassailable. But is anti-Semitism so rooted
in present-day culture or so present in the Christian mind-set
that international law is at best a feeble deterrent?

No clear answer to these difficult questions is available.
But world law has banned discriminatory conduct based on
race and has embodied this prohibition in the Covenant on the
Elimination of Racial Discrimination (CERD). The United
States and most other nations have ratified that treaty and participate in the work of the UN committee that monitors compliance with its provisions. The reports of that group and the
observed improvement of the signatory countries reveal many
signs that prejudice and bias predicated on race have been
ameliorated.

Could a similar United Nations supervisory group based
on religious freedom have comparable results? Even the nations most anxious to advance the objectives of CERD have
not arrived at a consensus that a similar legal arrangement to
promote religious freedom should be created. Do they fear
that anti-Semitism could not or would not be curbed or curtailed? Or do they fear that some Islamic countries would not
modify their Shari'a-based policies that stand in opposition to
some religious freedom norms of non-Islamic countries? Or—
one has to ask the ugly question—is the reticence caused by
vestiges of anti-Semitism that some nations do not want to acknowledge and confront?

The fate of the Jewish people since the Holocaust is possibly the strongest reason why the United Nations should pass
and have the nations ratify not merely a declaration but a

covenant on religious freedom. History shows that the Jewish people have always needed legal guarantees for the free exercise of their religion. In addition, the people of Israel deserve an international board that can give rulings of fairness on the theocratic elements of their government. For example, to what extent, if any, can a government controlled in part by a religious organization use the enforcement machinery of the state to advance religious objectives while possibly infringing on the faith of nonbelievers and others? The Israeli constitution deprives the non-Orthodox citizens of Israel of the political strength to effectively protest the actions of the religious elements in the incumbent government. If an international decree were issued in the case of Israel, such a ruling might well be applicable to the several Islamic countries where followers of non-Muslim creeds do not enjoy equal status with Muslims.

Reflection on the calamities that have been visited on the Jewish people despite the secular hopes developed and expanded since the Enlightenment can remind us that the commitments made by the rational nonreligious thinkers of the Enlightenment were frail. The contention of Enlightenment thinkers was that all religions, in their newly privileged state, would receive protection, and after centuries of ghettos and exclusions, the Jewish community welcomed the promise. But this new rational order could not save the Jews from Hitler's fanaticism, driven by concepts that found some support in age-old animosities in Christian thinking.

The slaughter of the Jews suggests that religious rights need to be integrated into the modern struggle for human rights. Indeed, the Holocaust can be taken as evidence that the struggle for human rights cannot be won without full attention to the authentic traditions of Judaism and Christianity. In other words, religions must be seen as the abiding allies of the struggle to protect human rights. The de facto exclusion of religion from the world of human rights has impoverished the effort—it has cut off many human rights from their roots. To ignore religious rights is to overlook the conceptual and historical sources of many individual and associational rights.

Further, the depreciation of religious rights has deepened the divide between Western and non-Western fundamental theories of rights. Many non-Western traditions, such as Islam, Hinduism, Buddhism, and some indigenous cultures, would not conceive of or accept a system of rights that excluded the right to religious practice. In nations holding this view, no system of rights that ignores the central place of religion can be adopted or respected. This silence about religion in Western concepts of human rights alienates many observers in non-Western nations. They look upon Western nations as seeking to impose a nontheistic set of values on the world, and the weakness and emptiness of those values was made tragically visible in the Holocaust—an event that left agonizing questions in non-Western nations as to why a nominally Christian country such as Germany should have murdered perhaps one-half of all the Jews in the world.

The Holocaust highlighted the hidden hypocrisy in the traditions and teachings of Christianity, whose sacred text and canons speak about respect for human rights. Judaism and Christianity contain in their teachings all the components of a strong human rights philosophy—respect for conscience, liberty, equality, tolerance, and love. But all these values were forgotten when a nation, and even a continent, acquiesced in the Holocaust.

It is ironic beyond all description that the Jewish people, whose religious traditions literally gave birth to the theory of human rights, should have been the victims of such an utter rejection of those rights. But that unspeakable injustice more than any other event was the cause and the occasion for the rebirth of human rights in the United Nations Charter and the Universal Declaration of Human Rights.

A World Tribunal and Jewish Religious Freedom

What protection can the international legal system offer to the Jewish people? One-third to one-half of the entire Jewish population was killed in the Holocaust. Of the remaining 14 million, some 5 million reside in Israel. The future availability of religious freedom for the Jewish people depends to some extent on the existence of a plan that will allow the people of Israel to abide in peace with the enjoyment of those human rights that have become the legacy and patrimony of every nation since 1948, when Israel was established. If the Jews in Israel and around the world do not obtain their right to the full exercise of religion, the whole system of the United Nations will have failed in one of its most fundamental tasks—to redeem the human race from the brutalities of the Holocaust.

If there were a covenant on religious freedom as there is for all of the major political and economic rights, Jews everywhere would have one additional potential remedy. If an optional protocol were added to such a covenant, individuals in nations that agreed to the protocol could appeal directly to an international commission or tribunal for relief. The simple availability of such a very public forum might deter governments in such places as Argentina from initiating or continuing hostile acts or attitudes against persons of Jewish heritage. The existence of such a new listening post for religious persecutions clearly would highlight the persistence of anti-Semitism, and might even convince the world that the silence that allowed the Holocaust to happen continues to permit anti-Semitism to poison the attitudes of countless people. Making discrimination of this kind an offense in world law could go further to inhibit nations from doing or allowing any conduct that could be perceived as anti-Semitic.

The United Nations commissions that process complaints based on violations of the major UN covenants on human rights have been bolstered by the International Criminal Court (ICC), which became operational in 2002. Designed as the permanent Nuremberg, the ICC will be able to comprehend, jail, and punish the Earth's worst malefactors, but without, alas, the participation of the United States, which has made clear its intent not to be bound by the treaty. The ICC is destined to become one of the most constructive and hopeful proposals ever devised to protect religious freedom and other precious privileges. This court will examine claims of only the most serious international crimes, such as genocide, and will not take action if the countries involved in the offense agree to take effective action.

It seems clear that serious offenses against internationally recognized human rights are rapidly becoming reportable and prosecutable in a growing list of nations. It is possible that most serious violations of human rights will soon be prosecuted in nations that have jurisdiction over the crime or over the offender. However, imposing a duty on nations by treaty to report serious crime based on anti-Semitism would allow one or more international commissions to investigate the charge. International juridical entities to which charges of anti-Semitism could be referred might be related to the United Nations, but one obstacle to this approach is seen in many persons' abiding distrust of the United Nations since the General Assembly's decree of October 17, 1975, that "Zionism is a form of racism and racial discrimination."

One likes to think that anti-Semitism, the omnipresent sin of the Christian centuries, has now been defined, castigated, and criminalized. The final necessary step would be a highly desirable world tribunal where offenses against any religious group would be punished. The religious freedom sought as a basic human right guaranteed by world law would finally become available to the Jewish communities everywhere in the world.

The shame, sorrow, and chagrin of all Christians since the Holocaust form the matrix for the modern movement for human rights and the need for an effective world tribunal that will seek to prevent anything like the Holocaust from occurring in the future. But one has to wonder whether all the aspirations and hopes for an effective system of protection of human rights are not somehow losing sight of the awful things that happened during the Nazi years in Europe. All those events are so painful that the family of nations seeks to put them out of mind by directing its attention to injustice elsewhere. But the world has not yet elevated the protection of religious freedom to the status obtained by other freedoms, such as the freedom of the press.

Why has the world been so reluctant to write and enforce a real covenant on the right to religious freedom? To create a real tribunal to detect and punish violations of religious freedom would require the world to pledge to eradicate all forms of anti-Semitism. Are the nations of the Earth ready to make such a commitment? Anti-Semitism has existed so long that one can wonder if the nations are ready to renounce it.

But irrespective of the existence of such an international covenant, Israel and the several effective Jewish nongovernmental organizations will continue to seek domestic remedies for past and present injustices attributable to anti-Semitism. Poland, for example, had 3.3 million Jews before World War II; 85 percent of them were murdered. Although the government of Poland has passed legislation providing for the restitution of property to the Catholic Church and other Christian entities, it has refused to do so in the case of the Jewish community. Such an injustice provides an opportunity for the international Jewish community to seek justice in the domestic legal system of Poland.

But can such efforts by international groups be truly effective? We simply do not know. Even savage assaults on large groups based on religion can flare up and disappear quickly, leaving the international community unable even to record the atrocities accurately. There is really no international machinery competent to record the murders by Indonesians of countless people in East Timor, for example, triggered at least partially by the Catholic faith of the East Timorese. We can look forward to the filling of that void by the ICC, at least in the very worst cases, such as outright genocide. Still, an active worldwide tribunal to adjudicate all claims based on religious freedom clearly has a role and a place not now being filled by any other governmental or international agency.

XIII
Questions of God
and Caesar

Of the many questions raised in a discussion of an international right to conscience, three are of lasting interest and importance: Can there be a world law regulating religious freedom at all? If so, should the right to religious freedom trump other rights? Finally, one must ask the question that spans the entire topic, affecting every part of it: Can Caesar and God ever truly coexist in peace?

Can There Be a World Law Regulating Religious Freedom?

It is disconcerting to realize that there is hardly even a vocabulary with which to talk about the relationship of religion and the state. The words of Christ directing that the things of Caesar be given to Caesar and the things of God be given to God may be the most descriptive and helpful of all the concepts, but even Christ's words do not seem helpful when we speak of religion in such nations as China and India. The simple distinction between God and Caesar seems less useful when it is subjected to modern analysis.

Adding modern notions of human rights to considerations of religion also seems to complicate the matter. When one says that there is a right to exercise religious freedom, the statement seems to presuppose that the government in question rules with the consent of the governed and can somehow be sanctioned for violating its promises, but this is not always the case. Also, generalized statements of a right to religious freedom do not account for the fact that governments have at least some authority to impose on the populace the duty to be loyal and obedient citizens. These considerations further complicate the formulation of a worldwide legal norm for the management of the right to worship God.

The best attempt at formulating some kind of legal code between God and Caesar is the 1981 United Nations Declaration on Religious Freedom. One can read this document (reproduced in Appendix A) and wonder what would happen if there were some world tribunal to interpret it. The legislative history of that document is not especially illuminating, but it does make clear the frustration of its authors and the prevailing consensus at the time of its drafting that the United Nations should accept the declaration and not press for a covenant or something more binding. That consensus may still exist, but the feeling a generation after the birth of the declaration is more one of acceptance of the status quo with the silent hope that the status of religious freedom does not deteriorate further. It is obvious, at least in the United States, that the tragic events of September 11, 2001, have further complicated the question of adopting a covenant to ensure the canons of religious freedom in Islamic nations.

There are several underlying issues and themes in the quest for religious freedom. First is the sovereignty of each nation. This ancient concept has often been exaggerated and abused, and it has clearly been complicated by the UN Charter and the Universal Declaration of Human Rights. Still, national leaders and their lawyers will argue strenuously that a sovereign nation has the right to prohibit any activity related to religion that, in the eyes or the imagination of reasonable leaders, could be threatening to the independence or the welfare of their nation. It is probably impossible to exaggerate the unilateral expansiveness of this concept. It goes back to the days of the Roman Empire, when countless Christians were executed because of their alleged disloyalty to the state.

How to curb potentially ruthless government restrictions is at the core of the struggle to maximize religious freedom. Many of the efforts of the human rights revolution are directed toward harmonizing the legislative needs of the state with the demands of sincere people of faith whose views collide with the government's demands. It is probably correct to note that these differences are inevitable, severe, and possibly irresolvable. But law—and increasingly international law—must at least try to resolve them. If international law does not make a sustained effort to resolve these clashes, they will only grow worse. The task appears increasingly formidable and even impossible, but to be silent is to allow government to become more demanding, imperious, and frightening.

Every generation has individuals and groups that claim some vision or mandate from above that requires them to refuse to obey governmental orders. Even from the perspective of a religious person, some of the demands of dissident religious sects seem bizarre and unreasonable, and there is a consensus that some of these claims must be rejected. Actions dangerous to life taken in the name of religion, for example, are always subject to close scrutiny by the courts. Accordingly, parents are never allowed to deny blood transfusions to their children in the name of an obscure passage in the Old Testament. Similarly, government policies require Christian Scientists not to rely purely on their faith in healing through God when they decide on treatments for their children.

But these are the easy cases. The more difficult ones arise out of religious beliefs or activities that appear to the government to pose a threat, however remote, to the state's sovereignty. The authority to combat such perceived threats claimed under sovereignty can be, at the state's option, almost indefinitely expandable and cruel. Every modern nation can become excessive in its restrictions of religious groups that seem to interfere with government. Yet every modern democracy has to allow the press to have its freedom, allow crowds to assemble to present their grievances, and allow ethnic groups to take measures to preserve their legacies. The conflict between these instincts of government might seem inherent, but nations do not always make great efforts to preserve the well-being of small religious groups in their midst. For example, all over Europe, Gypsies, Jehovah's Witnesses, the followers of Sun Myung Moon (the leader of the Unification Church), and similar groups (often pejoratively referred to as "sects") receive less than tolerance or acceptance.

Of course, Americans like to think that the U.S. Supreme Court has been generous to dissident religious groups, but that is not the view of spokesmen for such dissident groups as Native Americans, conscientious objectors, and Seventh-Day Adventists. The political leaders of the United States—like their counterparts in most other countries—do seek to protect religion, but elected officials prefer to be identified with a deity adopted by the government itself.

A dramatic example of this preference can be seen in the actions of the U.S. Senate after the Ninth Circuit Court of Appeals in California in a 2–1 ruling declared unconstitutional the words "under God" inserted in the Pledge of Allegiance to the Flag by the Congress in 1954. President Bush and a 99–0 vote by the Senate protested the ruling, stating in essence that "under God" was an invocation of the Supreme Being acceptable to the government, and indeed needed by the people of the United States. Even those who might otherwise object to the decision spoke vaguely about the acceptability of a "ceremonial theism." The incident illustrates the deep-down reality that the United States government wants to be identified with *some* God. If challenged, government authorities refer to the words of George Washington in his farewell address: "Of all the dispositions and habits which lead to political prosperity, religion and morality are indispensable supports."

Can a formula be devised by which the worldwide boundaries between God and Caesar can be determined? That is the task outlined in the article "A Draft Model Law on Freedom of Religion with Commentary" by two U.S. academics, Dinah Shelton and Alexander Kiss, in *Religious Human Rights in Global Perspective: Legal Perspectives,* edited by Johan D. van der Vyver and John Witte Jr. This well-researched article proceeds on the assumption that there is an "international recognition that views about the sacred play a special role in every society and should be protected by law" (561).

The draft model law in its statement of legislative purposes reminds national governments of their duty to comply with relevant international treaties and with customary international law. Article 1 also requires nations to "ensure the separation of the state and religion." It is by no means clear, however, that customary international law requires that separation in any of its many variations.

The authors concede that they have followed the "most expansive international statements." But as one reads the model law's seventeen articles, one has to wonder if a broad range of nations would ever be willing to adopt them. They might if they were under constant pressure from the world community and from nongovernmental organizations, but China and several of the Islamic nations would still be likely to insist on many reservations. The question, therefore, is whether the countries that follow the Judeo-Christian tradition should focus on the United Nations Declaration on Religious Freedom and the proposed model law and seek to have them clarified and updated into a United Nations covenant binding on all members.

At the moment, the international human rights community does not appear to have the determination to press forward toward the creation of a covenant. However, the entire human rights community of nongovernmental organizations is getting stronger all the time, and the moral power of this community should not be underestimated. Furthermore, although some of the seventeen articles of the draft model law would no doubt pose lasting problems for some countries, there does appear to be a growing consensus on several issues, such as the desirability of broadening the definition of religious freedom.

Article 3 of the draft model law guarantees the right to change one's religion. One would think that this tenet, now a part of customary international law for many years, would be accepted, yet it has not been universally recognized. The Sudanese Criminal Act of 1991, for example, provides that any Muslim who urges others to renounce the creed of Islam or who publicly declares his renunciation thereof commits apostasy, a crime punishable by death.

Article 4 seeks to protect from compulsion all who believe or refuse to believe. This guarantee is, one would hope, accepted by all nations. But a common sticking point is the question of compelling a citizen to perform armed military service contrary to his or her religion or belief. The proposed model law seems to finesse this point by stipulating that "no one may refuse to perform in unarmed military service for humanitarian purposes or in the interest of the general welfare." This provision probably goes against a minority view that countries should introduce alternate, acceptable forms of service for conscientious objectors.

In the realm of education, excusal provisions are recommended so that students are not compelled to participate in religious activities or receive religious instruction. The draft model law guarantees the right of all religious groups to disseminate publications, maintain religious institutes, acquire places of worship, and train leaders for religious groups. The confidentiality of communications made to religious authorities is specifically protected, as is the right to reasonable accommodation in scheduling for manifestations of religion or belief.

Article 6 states broadly that "the state is secular and has no official or established religion." Thus "no religion or religious organization may receive any privileges from the state nor exercise any political authority." However, the state may financially support "the medical activities and the educational, charitable and social service of religious organizations provided this is done without any discrimination." The draft model law also provides that "public authorities are prohibited from involvement in the selection or role of religious officials, the structure of religious organisms or the organization of worship or other rights."

One could argue that Article 6 goes against the United Nations Declaration on Religious Freedom by insisting that all forms of state-established religion must be phased out. Relics of state religions remain in several nations. In England, for example, prime ministers appoint bishops and the House of Lords contains twenty-six Anglican bishops. The Parliament can rule on doctrinal and liturgical matters. Although these ancient practices arouse little protest, they can be seen to discriminate against minority religions.

Article 6's provision that nations cannot impart any privileges to religions would presumably require Austria, Denmark, Germany, Norway, and Finland to cease collecting taxes for religious bodies. A similar duty would be placed on Libya, Somalia, and other Islamic countries whose constitutions proclaim Islam as the religion of the state. In Sudan, the head of state is required to be a Muslim. Similar laws enforcing the subordination of all religious bodies to the government can be found in many nations, and the model law would stand in opposition to all such instances. The draft model law also in essence accepts Article 6 of the U.S. Constitution, which states that no religious test shall ever be applied to candidates for public office.

Article 6 tries to protect religious organizations from discrimination, but it may not reach organizations that a nation declares to be "dangerous." Religious groups have been declared "dangerous" in countries such as Angola, Ethiopia, Ghana, Mozambique, Uganda, Tanzania, and Zaire. China's constitution provides that "no one may use religion or promote activities detrimental to the social order, injurious to citizens' health or liable to impair the health of citizens or the educational system of the state." It also states that "religious bodies or religious affairs are not subject to any foreign domination" and similarly affirms that "religious groups and activities may not be controlled by foreign groups."

Although Article 6 of the draft model law permits certain

restrictions on religious practices, the commentary on the model law states that the burden should be "on the government to demonstrate by clear evidence the reasons for limiting religious liberty."

Articles 7 through 12 of the draft model law urge the autonomy of religious groups and provide that schools can be created under religious auspices, but do not take up the question of government financing.

Article 13 takes up the taxation of religious groups. No exemption is required, except that religious groups should be able to receive tax-exempt gifts in the same way that nonprofit organizations do. The dangers inherent in the taxation of religions are noted, however, from inflating or minimizing the valuation of religious property to manipulating the definition of what qualifies as a religion for tax purposes. The commentary on Article 13 raises the basic question whether exemption from taxation should be required, but gives no answer except to warn of the potential dangers of allowing governments to decide whether religious units should be taxed and, if so, at what rate.

Articles 14 through 17 relate to topics that seem to be outdated. For example, claims of blasphemy are considered here. Laws against blasphemy were originally designed to protect dominant religions from affront and attack, but punishments for blasphemy appear to have passed into history, except in such nations as Pakistan. Would a less stringent law prohibiting public insults to religion be useful or enforceable? In the vast literature on religious freedom one finds little, if any, support for enforcement or reintroduction of laws against blasphemy.

One would like to welcome the United Nations Declaration on Religious Freedom and the proposed draft model law as great steps forward, but they seem to be imprecise in the proposed regulations of an area that is itself not clearly defined and not easily regulated. Take the issue of proselytism.

A specific interest of Christians is their desire to be able to travel abroad and spread their gospel. Christ set forth the duty to evangelize in language that is clear and compelling. The Catholic and Protestant churches have created vast networks in scores of nations colonized by the countries of Europe in order to fulfill their mission to convert. Of course, that vast spiritual enterprise has been seriously reversed and retarded in China and several other countries hostile to Christianity.

Christians must ask whether they have some right under the new human rights doctrine of international law to preach their gospel in non-Christian countries. Of course, Christians do not want to press too vigorously for a restitution of that right. They recognize that some non-European nations feel strongly against Western countries—especially against those that send missionaries to convert their populations. The Chinese dramatically demonstrated their disdain for missionaries in the many martyrdoms of Christians carried out in the Boxer Rebellion of 1900. Japan, India, and other nations have created a list of such martyrs, and they are regularly recalled in the liturgy of the Catholic Church.

Christian missionaries are still permitted in most Latin American countries. The Maryknoll order, established in the United States for the precise purpose of evangelizing China, turned to Latin America after China closed its doors to missionaries after the Communists took power in 1949. Some of the basic presumptions of missionary work have been altered since that time, but the fundamental question remains: Should international law state that Christian missionaries of all kinds have a right to enter a foreign nation in the same way that industrialists, academics, and artists can enter? The draft model law would seem to say yes, but jurists and the promoters of international human rights hesitate to insist that sovereign nations be forced to admit foreign apostles of a religion that has never been welcomed.

Questions abound. Do the people of China have a right to keep out voices that are in their view "un-Chinese"? Or do Christians and Muslims, following the mandates of their religions, have a right to explain their beliefs in persuasive ways to persons with a totally different heritage?

It is possible that the problem will be solved, at least in part, by missionaries' adoption of the techniques that are transforming the way the whole world learns. The conflict may also be eased if the resisting nations simply acknowledge the undeniable fact that no borders are secure against ideas and information. People in the remotest areas of the Earth can hear CNN, the Voice of America, the BBC, and perhaps soon the sounds of the Gospel radiated from Christian centers in China, India, or Africa, or even the West.

When one is exploring the possible rights conferred by international law on persons of faith, it is also fair and just to contemplate the right of nonbelievers to be protected from voices with messages that are not compatible with their deepest convictions. Whatever right they may have in this area also implicates the right of once-colonized countries to erase the messages left by its former colonizers.

I remember a dramatic scene I witnessed in South Africa when I lectured there one summer shortly after the abolition of apartheid. An eloquent law student proclaimed his desire to expel everything that the colonizers had brought to South Africa, including Christianity. I had a difficult time trying to disengage Christianity from the many injustices imposed on the black people of South Africa. The law student's position raises the core issue whether Christian missionaries have a right to go to these nations once colonized by European countries. Should the people of those former colonies have a right to keep out Christians who desire to preach to them about Christianity?

The questions are sprawling and are intermingled with issues connected with globalization and the right of countries to maintain their cultural autonomy. China, of course, was never truly colonized, so it does not fall into this category. We need different rules for this nation, which now contains some 20 percent of the human race. This is a concrete example of the challenges confronting Christians who, because of their faith and conscience, feel themselves called to preach their faith in the East, Latin America, Africa, and elsewhere.

Indeed, the Mormon faith puts strong pressure on its young adherents to spend up to two years doing missionary work somewhere outside the United States. The Church of Jesus Christ of Latter Day Saints (LDS) has almost 12 million members, half of whom live outside the United States. Its membership has skyrocketed.

The LDS has always embraced religious freedom. In a general assembly in 1835, Mormon leaders proclaimed their ardent belief in religious freedom and in enactment of laws to guarantee that freedom. Nevertheless, the Mormons were persecuted in the United States, possibly more than any other religious body. That persecution ended domestically before 1900, but the improvement in their situation at home did not deter them from sending missionaries to scores of other countries. Today the LDS has a presence in some 160 countries. Currently their missionaries are men between the ages of 19 and 26 (75 percent), single women (17 percent), and retired couples (8 percent).

The LDS seeks to maintain diplomatic relations with the

countries to which it sends missionaries, and those contacts have improved in recent years in such countries as Greece, Portugal, Poland, and the countries of the former Yugoslavia. Although Mormon leaders have sought the right to hold open meetings and to own property, they have not made policy recommendations to the United Nations about religious freedom. However, the LDS did conduct a conference in 2000 at Brigham Young University to explore international law and religion. The conference examined the implications of the 1981 United Nations Declaration on Religious Freedom.

The LDS has met resistance in Eastern Europe. The church has operated extensively in Poland and in some countries of the former Yugoslavia, but in 1997 it experienced difficulties in Russia under new laws passed to curtail religious freedom.

The Mormons have had difficulties obtaining visas for some countries, such as Latvia and Croatia. They face other obstacles in Bulgaria and Romania, and in Armenia, Mormons, along with other potential missionaries, face a law that forbids proselytizing by any church other than the Armenian Apostolic Church. Even in Belgium and France the LDS has been impeded by legislation designed to curb religious sects. The Mormon presence was complicated by Germany's refusal to recognize the Church of Scientology.

The LDS, like many Christian denominations, would like to proselytize in China. The Mormons now have 40,000 members there, more than half of them in Hong Kong. The Mormons are almost completely absent from the Muslim world.

The fact that the LDS continues to face these obstacles despite its zeal and dedication to quiet diplomacy illustrates the concrete problems faced by Christian missionaries. The United Nations Declaration on Religious Freedom and the proposed draft model law are aimed at protecting and enhancing the deep desire of the Mormons and countless other religious bodies to share their faith and their tradition with people who have never heard the Gospel of Jesus Christ.

It is clear, however, that some missionaries through the centuries have abused their role and have not treated the local population with the deep respect it deserves. It is also clear that throughout history Christian churches have aided colonial powers in inappropriate ways. But today the scene is almost totally different. The governments of the non-European members of the United Nations are trying to cope with the churches they have inherited. Although recent additions to the United Nations may have some gratitude to the churches established by England, France, Spain, and the other colonizers, the surging populations of Africa and Asia do not think kindly of missionaries coming to convert them to Christianity now.

When one surveys the role of religion in the vast world of formerly colonized countries, the mandate of international law may seem to be peripheral, but it is not. Since 1945 the international law of human rights has integrated its core moral concepts into domestic laws around the world. The sovereignty of nations has been sharply narrowed and the primacy of human rights has been elevated everywhere. Among these near-universal rights is the freedom to believe or not to believe—everyone's rights in that area are guaranteed.

In connection with the right of missionaries to proselytize in foreign lands, everyone should remember that the citizens of those countries also have a right to adhere to their own faith or lack of it. The people in Africa and elsewhere have yet to articulate their right to adhere to their present faiths, but international law may eventually require protections for domestic non-Christian groups to counterbalance the right of religious groups such as the Mormons to evangelize. In other words, governments must not offer direct or indirect assistance to outside Christian or Muslim missionaries seeking to convert their citizens.

Could there be a struggle over the next few decades between the zealots of Christianity and the disciples of the Muslim faith? No one can predict, but the faith of Christians and the tenets of Islam are held passionately by millions of people, and both have international law on their side. That law gives a right to proselytize to all groups and forbids the state to side openly with any religion. It must be, however, that at present the legal machinery is ill equipped to maintain the balance between governments and religion.

The international legal community of academics and activists on human rights has created a whole new legal and moral community since 1945. This community seems to be a force of growing strength and intensity. Yet it seems to have only a few adherents in the world of Islam.

Respect for religious freedom seems to be instinctual, deep, and powerful, but it has not yet flowered and matured like the right to freedom of the press or speech. Ultimately, however, religious liberty may grow to become a right more important than many of the others recognized by the human race since the end of World War II.

Should Religious Freedom Trump Other Rights?

The thrust of international human rights law in respect to religious freedom is that the freedom to worship as one's conscience dictates is unique and should be as inviolable as circumstances permit. Of course, it is not clear that the right to religious freedom should supersede or trump all other rights, but the contemporary law on human rights speaks about religious freedom in tones that are almost reverent. The consensus is remarkable. Almost irresolvable problems arise, however, when a rule imposed by government is openly at odds with the deep-seated desire of people to live according to their deepest instincts.

Such a problem is the rigid rule in China that most couples may have only one child. The government's rationale is, of course, that a lack of space and resources necessitates the curbing of population growth. The whole world knows the awful consequences—there are many abortions, and, because of a common preference for sons, female fetuses are disproportionately aborted. A large number of girls are abandoned, although some are ultimately adopted by couples in the West. In a narrow sense, this complex problem could be said not to involve religious freedom as such. But clearly every religious body in the world and every religious person feels that the fundamental rights of spouses to manage their family in accord with their beliefs is compromised by the one-child requirement.

If a world commission or court existed to hear complaints about the limitations on religious freedom, what could the judges do? The complainants presumably would include Chinese parents or future parents. They would assert that their freedom to have the number of children they desire should be protected by various provisions in international human rights law, including the provisions that ban governments from requiring citizens to violate the tenets of their religion, the dictates of their conscience, and the callings of their most fundamental convictions.

A world tribunal on religious freedom would have to evaluate the justifications offered by the government in Beijing for its radical invasion into the lives of Chinese citizens. Is Beijing correct in concluding that the only way to control the density of China's population is to restrict the number of children to one per couple in the crowded urban areas? The judges would have to assess the proof offered by the Chinese government. It could be that the world community would require China to expand its habitable areas or—as a radical alternative—permit some Chinese citizens to emigrate to other nations.

Any remedy for the millions of families in China who feel that their basic rights are being denied will not be easy. But even if the parents who brought claims did not follow religion as such, they could qualify for relief if their desire to have more than one child derived from "belief" or "conscience"—both protected by provisions in the international law of religious freedom.

Apart from the problems confronting the Chinese family, the pressure placed by the Chinese government on women to obtain abortions is of distinct concern. The feminists of the world may hold that women have a basic right to abort non-viable fetuses, but they are equally adamant that no government should be able to force a woman to abort the child she desires.

The lamentable situation in China intersects with the global conflict over abortion. Some 40 million abortions are performed in the world every year, and it is clear to many people that steps to diminish this number are desirable. Information about birth control should be available everywhere; indeed, this is one of the rights guaranteed in the Convention on the Elimination of Discrimination against Women, a treaty ratified by the vast majority of countries in the world, but not the United States. If this right were widely recognized and respected, the number of unplanned and unwanted pregnancies would, at least theoretically, diminish.

If an international tribunal on religious freedom existed,

it could recommend that the rights of women everywhere include the power to control their reproductive capacity in ways that are congruent with their religious convictions. It is not clear, however, that the majority of nations would subscribe to the belief that couples should have access to contraceptive measures. The Islamic nations, along with India and other countries, can be very restrictive in their views on birth control and abortion.

This diversity of views highlights the fact that there is no consensus on women's rights and abortion approaching the near-universal agreement on rights such as freedom of the press. The profound difficulty over the question of abortion is probably one of the major reasons why the international community has never pressed for a binding treaty on the rights of religious believers. It is possible, however, that the majority of nations will reach a consensus that abortion should be restricted to extraordinary cases such as rape, incest, or a serious threat to the life of the mother. If this narrow view became customary international law, would nations such as the United States be forced to follow suit?

These troublesome questions have inhibited nations from seeking global reviews of issues that are hotly contested. Despite all these difficulties, the declarations and covenants related to human rights emphasize that the freedom to practice one's religion is different from and higher than all the other human rights that have been incorporated in the body of customary international law.

Religious believers are obviously inclined to provide legal protection for the freedom to worship God. But even non-believers sense that it is wrong for a government to compel its citizens to go against their firmly held views on what their god requires or forbids them to do. For centuries governments have been repressing or silencing religions or, more likely in modern days, ignoring them. In some future golden age of human rights, governments and the international community may act with generosity and tenderness to all religions, especially to those that are unpopular or controversial. Until that happy time arrives, what can the family of nations do to implement the right to religious freedom?

The United Nations Human Rights Committee is one of several units at the United Nations that monitor compliance with the International Covenant on Civil and Political Rights (ICCPR). The committee evaluates the periodic reports of nations that have become signatories of the ICCPR. This committee is one means by which the world can expand religious freedom in the absence of a similar UN committee to supervise the fulfillment of demands for religious freedom, because the committee could exercise jurisdiction over such cases. However, the Human Rights Committee seems to want to stay out of the tortuous struggles over religion in places such as Northern Ireland and the Middle East. Petitioners rarely bring disputes about religious rights to the UN Committee on Human Rights, because there are few precedents for decisions involving religious disputes. It concentrates instead on political issues brought to its attention by the member nations or by personalities in the world press.

The UN Commission on Human Rights has repeatedly been lobbied by China to stay out of human rights issues in that country. In fact, the consortium of nations loyal to China has been remarkably successful through the years in getting a majority of nations to table complaints made against China. However, if a separate UN committee on religious freedom were formed pursuant to a new covenant on the freedom of religion, it could take up issues such as China's one-child policy.

Beijing would no doubt continue to lobby to keep its practices off the agenda, but China might be less likely to succeed with a religious committee, or even with the existing Commission on Human Rights, if that commission chose to turn its attention to religious freedom.

Until an international tribunal to monitor religious freedom comes into existence, the world community will continue to define and refine the concept that the right to worship in one's own way is something precious and inviolable. Many of the international declarations recognizing religious freedom use and stress the term "conscience." It is truly amazing to see that all the nations that adopted the Universal Declaration of Human Rights and the Covenant on Human Rights agreed on the use of the term "conscience." There is an astonishing consensus in the human family that every person is required to follow the voice of conscience. That consensus seems to be based on the idea that there is a voice within that comes from God or some transcendent force, and that failure to follow it will bring guilt and self-condemnation. The world understands and admires individuals such as St. Thomas More, who accepted execution rather than accept King Henry VIII as the spiritual leader of England.

Humanity is less sympathetic in judging governments that require a citizen to go against all his convictions and his conscience by submitting to the mandate of having only one child. The word "conscience" offers a clear warning to everyone: conscience should *never* be violated. There can be discussions and quibbles about the conscience that is ill informed or unscrupulous or unreasonable, but when the question is a matter of a person's compelling religious beliefs, men and women everywhere agree that concessions should be made to accommodate conscience.

It is probably going too far to assert that religious freedom trumps all other human rights. Human rights are indivisible and all are equally precious. The conclusion of the 1993 United Nations World Conference on Human Rights held in Vienna makes that principle crystal-clear. However, there still is something uniquely offensive in a state policy that requires a person to violate the imperious demands of conscience.

Until a global commission can sort out and rule on the clashes between the asserted needs of governments and the claims of religious freedom, theologians and agnostics should conduct a dialogue on the almost incredible fact that, in a world of 6 billion people, there is a remarkable consensus that every government should respect the conscience of every human being. This fact should be kept in mind as the world searches for some institution that will protect the right and duty of every human being to follow the dictates of his or her conscience.

An additional way for the family of nations to protect religious freedom is to foster intensified dialogue between organized religions of all forms. As we have seen, the major religions of the world have been active and articulate in their quest for an expansion of the intersections between religion and human rights. Of course, the feeling is widespread that organized religions seek to protect their own interests even when their actions arguably violate or constrict religious freedoms, but this belief is ill founded. Both the World Council of Churches and the Catholic Church in Vatican II have rejected self-serving positions in the name of preserving individual rights. Indeed, an examination of the world's religions demonstrates that, notwithstanding their individual interests, virtually all religious traditions seek to strengthen the expansion and the enforcement of human rights.

Can Caesar and God Coexist in Peace?

This book will undoubtedly be criticized for apparent contradictions, omissions, and ambiguities. The very concept of talking about religious freedom and world law bristles with concepts that seemingly do not cohere.

The subject of the proper relationship between churches and the state is old, mysterious, and unfathomable. It has been made more so by the sudden recognition of a right never considered before the mid–twentieth century— the right to enjoy religious freedom. It is almost a fairy tale. The fact that the right has not been seriously protected by the United Nations and the world community should probably not be surprising, because the notion of an international governmental unit guaranteeing the free exercise of religion is a dream that the present generation has seldom entertained.

The idea of preserving and protecting religious freedom is particularly sensitive because three of the world's major religions—Christianity, Islam, and Judaism—claim that God himself entered into history and spoke to his people. Christianity is even more astounding, as it claims that God became a man "like unto us in all things sin excepted," as St. Paul put it. The claims of Christianity become even more spectacular when that religion asserts that Christ the man rose from the dead—the only person in all history to have done so. There are no precedents or legal categories to handle such a claim. Indeed, there are hardly words to explain how the Son of God could become a man and yet remain fully divine.

This book will also trouble some readers because at the age of twenty-three its author took the vows of poverty, chastity, and obedience as a Jesuit. Some will point out that I can hardly claim to be an objective observer of the state of reli-

gions in the world. This observation will have particular force
for the millions of persons who have never had instruction in
any religion and who are deeply skeptical of all supernatural
claims. Such persons probably want to reject the assertions
found everywhere in international law that religious freedom
is precious and must be protected.

The distaste and even distrust that so many people have
for any organized religion is probably attributable to the failures of many religions to live up to their stated purpose of loving God's poor and serving justice. When religious figures
such as St. Francis of Assisi, Pope John XXIII, and Mother
Teresa live up to this ideal, they usually receive universal admi-
ration and love. But the thought of the men who loosed the
Crusades and the Inquisition on the world in the name of religion reminds us how cruel religious institutions can be.

Much of the vast literature on the relationship of religion
and government recalls that all the religions of the world
preach that everyone owes the duty of love to every other child
of God. Both friends and enemies of religion claim that there
would be no strife between religions and government if religious institutions just stayed within their mission to preach
love. But this pious wish is hopelessly unrealistic, because religions are by their nature intended to create cultures, even civilizations. Religions strive to create a community where believers can love God and each other, and such a community
inevitably requires laws, rules, and traditions. As a result, rela-
tionships grow and develop between the religious community
and the secular government. Even a theocracy requires a civil
government of some kind.

Many commentators, fearing the domination of either
government or the church in a society, have sought, in essence,

to privatize churches and the voice of religion. It is thought that under such a scheme, the churches avoid the domination of government and the government is not controlled by the churches. This was a nice ideal for Roger Williams and Thomas Jefferson, but in the pluralistic, secularized, big-government society of today, strict separation can cause churches to become marginalized.

The reality is that the newly globalized world needs a formula that will allow, and indeed inspire, churches to be more vigorous in carrying out their essential mission. What this mission is exactly is the subject of constant study by Christians and others in the United States. The churches appreciate— perhaps more than others—the awful injustices in a world where 800 million of God's children are chronically malnourished. People of faith cringe when they realize that the human family spends $900 billion each year on arms and armaments. Religious groups of all kinds want to shout and proclaim from the housetops the injustices and the cruelty that men are inflicting on each other. However, religious groups currently have no place at the table when decisions are made that affect a world where wars continue, starvation grows, illiteracy increases, and injustices of all kinds multiply.

Churches recognize that they must be more than social welfare agencies, but they also know that they cannot become prayer groups isolated from the agonizing problems of their society. Faith calls religiously affiliated groups to spread their messages, and therefore to do more than only act as Good Samaritans, silently extending charity to individuals who are victimized by society. However, the messages of churches differ: religious organizations do not always speak with a united voice, even on some central issues. One result is that political authorities do not always heed the messages of churches. It is clear that politicians do not want to be admonished for failing to follow the advice of religious groups, but the disunity among the religious voices in the United States and elsewhere allows elected officials to deny having received any clear advice.

The international voice of religious groups such as the World Council of Churches is often strong, but, unfortunately, such groups are not linked directly with Roman Catholic bodies or with non-Christian organizations. Although no worldwide coalition of religions exists at present, when one reflects on the state of religious freedom in the world, it is difficult not to imagine some sort of alliance between the religious traditions of the world.

Even if no linking of the religions of the world is feasible, one would think that an international dialogue among the faiths on the planet should be possible, but even this is not certain. In such a dialogue, Christians would hold very firmly that God himself and his Son created a religion that the Creator and Redeemer certified as the real Church of God. However, the Catholic Church and many other religions have recognized that the Spirit of God speaks in multiple places and that he wishes the salvation of everyone. Protestants, having participated in a wide variety of past dialogues with Catholics, Orthodox Christians, and Muslims, would also be likely to join in some worldwide alliance of all believers. The role for Buddhists and Hindus is more complicated.

Could the major religious organizations of the world come together in the name of religious freedom? It is possible that they could rely on the United Nations Declaration on Religious Freedom and the growing body of literature on the legal, juridical, and political aspects of guaranteeing freedom of religion throughout the world. The international ferment over human rights and the overwhelming momentum behind globalization could jointly provide the incentive to the world religious community to unite for the purpose of expediting the advent of religious freedom. At present, however, there appears to be no independent inducement that would produce such a meeting.

Of course, it is not clear that the shapers of international law would be eager to have religious leaders become actors on the world stage. It is true that the movers and shakers of international law who are involved in the development of the World Trade Organization are more and more active with human rights groups that seek to guarantee the rights of workers. However, any potential coming together of religious groups to secure religious freedom would not on its face be attractive to those who each day seek to improve the work of such agencies as the World Bank.

The human rights groups around the world might well see the potential for the advancement of their work in an alliance of some kind with religious organizations. The vast work of protecting internationally recognized human rights requires the creation of a seamless web, and strengthening religious freedom by creative means would almost necessarily validate the state of all human rights. Guaranteeing the right of religious groups to meet and organize in a nation such as Malaysia would clearly give a lift to the promoters of all other human rights.

In order to form coalitions, the essential thing that religious groups have to do is to make themselves more attractive to their neighbors. On a broader scale, religious groups must demonstrate that they are operating out of sincere love and not for narrow sectarian objectives. This is easy to say, but it must be remembered that the daily work of religious organizations is not by its nature designed to be attractive to those of another religion or of no religion.

Although the topic of securing religious freedom for everyone in the world seems overwhelming, there are some guidelines for persons involved in humanity's historic struggle to emancipate religious believers while not disadvantaging nonbelievers. I offer these thoughts for actors in religious bodies, governments, and nongovernmental agencies.

1. *Religious bodies.* Persons working in religious organizations must urge believers to be restrained in any activity that might be perceived as an effort to impose their views on others or on governments. We must remember the adage that when a miracle occurs, no explanation for believers is necessary, while for nonbelievers no explanation is possible.

All religious bodies should recognize that the imposition of their beliefs on others goes against the sense of personal dignity and autonomy that is inculcated in the modern soul when international human rights are respected. The Declaration on Religious Freedom issued by the Second Vatican Council mentions this idea several times and in several ways. The essence of freedom of religion is "immunity from coercion" and the belief that a concept cannot be imparted "except by virtue of its own truth" (paragraph 1). Note 51 asserts that the declaration is "a final renouncement and repudiation by the Church of all means and measures of coercion in matters religious."

All of the many references to religious freedom in the documents of the United Nations assume and imply that religious bodies will refrain from any measures that could be deemed to be coercive. The memory of "rice Christians"—the term applied to Asians who briefly espoused Christianity in order to obtain the food and comforts offered by missionaries—overshadows the topic of religious freedom in secular and sacred literature. The widespread practice of herding people into a faith by means approaching coercion has been repudiated by governments and by churches. At the same time, Muslim nations look upon anyone born into that religion as belonging irreversibly to that group.

Catholics were warned by the declarations of the Second Vatican Council that any hint of coercion in their dealings with Christians or non-Christians is inappropriate. Protestant sources have been saying the same thing for many years. In addition, the tenor of Catholic-Protestant relations has recently become more amicable than at any time since the Reformation. A clarification of international law on the full meaning of religious freedom would help both groups to achieve the fullness of freedom that they want for themselves and for each other.

Catholics should find it particularly congenial to carry out the directives of the Universal Declaration of Human Rights, because Monsignor Angelo Roncalli, who subsequently became Pope John XXIII, collaborated in its preparation when he was the papal nuncio in Paris in 1948. Sean MacBride, human rights leader and Nobel laureate, affirmed that the future pope participated closely with René Cassin, the principal author of the Universal Declaration.

2. *Government actors.* Governments have much to learn from international law's conferral of religious freedom on all ecclesiastical bodies. For centuries, local and national governments have been in the habit of using and misusing local religious groups for their own political objectives, but those days should now be happily at an end.

The 1981 Universal Declaration on Religious Freedom is designed to curb the subordination of religion to the objectives of government. Article 4 of the declaration comments that all states "shall" prevent and eliminate discrimination on the grounds of religion or belief "in all fields of civil, economic, political, social and cultural life." Those broad terms were chosen to tell governments that checkerboard patterns in housing or business based on religious affiliation must be phased out.

The UN declaration makes it clear that no exclusion or preference based on religion or belief can be allowed. Its language is unmistakable: no nation can grant a higher or lower status to Christians, Muslims, Jews, or any other group on the sole basis of religion. Nor may a government exclude any person from any position in the nation on the basis of "religion or belief." Indeed, the ban extends to discrimination by "groups or persons or person."

Many governments would hesitate to subscribe to the demands of the United Nations Declaration on Religious Freedom for fear that minority religious groups would press forward vigorously with demands for equality. Other nations would assert that as sovereign states they do not need the prodding of the declaration. But if the declaration ever became accepted, and certainly if it achieved the status of customary international law, there could be at least a minor revolution in the way governments look upon religious organizations.

Some observers will wonder whether the acceptance of the UN Declaration on Religious Freedom would make any difference. Would the war between Catholics and Protestants in Northern Ireland abate? Would the Kurds be treated differently? Would Christians in India be granted more tolerance? Would Christians in Sudan receive more acceptance? The only answer is that every law curbing discrimination and intolerance changes the world climate. Like civil rights laws in the United States, a world law protecting religious freedom would make discriminatory conduct less acceptable and eventually, it is hoped, make such conduct unthinkable.

Governments would be even less willing to agree to this reform if they believed that they would eventually be pressured to commit to treaty provisions allowing individual citizens to appeal an alleged denial of religious freedom to a UN tribunal. The spokespersons for some nations would protest the creation of a United Nations Commission on Religious Freedom on the basis that religious freedom, unlike the freedom of the press, defies definition or adjudication. Religion, they would argue, is so intertwined with culture and language that it cannot be realistically made the subject of a court decree. The argument has merit, but if there is to be an international right to faith, there will have to be some way of evaluating compliance.

Every nation has to search for its core identity through its legislature and its courts. The place of religion in the national culture is always a question of great concern, and every country has a unique history of its relation to religion. How a nation defines religious freedom is the end result of a very complicated process.

The United States is no exception. The U.S. Supreme Court coped with the issue in its 1952 6–3 ruling in *Zorach*. In 1948, in its 8–1 decision in *McCollum*, the Court had banned classes in religion for students in public schools, even when the students had the written permission of their parents. The national protest over this decision had been vehement. In *Zorach*, the Supreme Court was called upon to rule on the constitutionality of religious education conducted by public schools but held off of school premises. The Supreme Court allowed this arrangement, stating in a decision written by Justice William Douglas that "we are a religious people whose institutions presuppose the existence of a supreme being." If other nations felt the same way, they would theoretically be prepared to accept a worldwide monitor to guarantee that their people could perpetuate their status as a "religious people."

3. *Nongovernmental actors.* A third group of spokespersons is the rapidly growing community of nongovernmental organizations (NGOs) devoted to human rights. The scope of involvement and the intensity of devotion of this new community are amazing. NGOs fight for the rights of women, children, refugees, the disabled, and other groups of victims. They were omnipresent at the United Nations World Conference on Human Rights in Vienna in 1993, and since then they have evidenced even greater levels of involvement and influence.

These groups are so committed to their goals that it is not appropriate to fault them. It does seem, however, that their interest in religious freedom has not developed in the same way as their attention to other issues. This is quite understandable, inasmuch as there is not yet a United Nations covenant on religious freedom, only a declaration. At the same time, the neglect of religious freedom pulls apart the seamless garment of which all human rights are part. If nations are not placed under pressure for the mishandling of religious freedom, they may be less likely to comply with their duties under other pledges solemnly made to the United Nations. In addition, it must be noted that if religious dissidents are allowed to speak out and act on behalf of human rights, a whole new army of friends of human rights will have been created.

Some of the most vigorous NGOs devoted to human rights are affiliated with Jewish organizations. From the World Jewish Congress down to the local level, Jewish-affiliated NGOs have led the way. These groups were uniquely successful in their efforts to bring relief to the 3 million Soviet Jews, half or more of whom were finally allowed to emigrate to the United States, Israel, and elsewhere.

There are probably no Christian human rights organizations as influential as those of Jewish origin. Christian groups have depended on an ever-broader array of NGOs devoted to human rights. However, a coalition of Jewish and Christian organizations devoted to the enlargement of freedom could be uniquely effective. Christians have the additional motive of seeking to offer atonement for the Holocaust, which occurred in Christian countries.

People of faith tend to see the will of God in human events. At the same time, many religious people want to take up secular, even violent means to stop evil things from harming religious institutions. The approval of violent means by the Christian Church has at times been so pervasive that before the Middle Ages, the Church helped to devise seven conditions for a "just" war. But this thinking is now possibly obsolete.

People of faith started the Crusades and other "holy wars" to protect the Church. Today Catholics feel chagrin and guilt for many actions taken through the centuries to protect and extend the Church. Pope John Paul II has publicly apologized for some eighty acts of the Church through the centuries. Some of those mistakes were made in the name of advancing the faith or curbing the "infidels." Many of them were designed to, and did, deny or blunt the victims' religious freedom.

The Catholics, like all Christians, have altered in many ways their ideas about what actions to advance the faith are legitimate. But despite this change in Christian attitude, past misdeeds linger in the history books and in the living and continuing memory of millions of people who regard the acts as indefensible. Of course, this history also affects the attitudes of the over 1 billion Catholics living everywhere in the world who ask how their church could ever have used the power of Caesar to advance the objectives of God. Of course, Protestants are also forced to reconcile the fact that their religion has sometimes used similar tactics. In the end, wars against heretics and comparable measures have left today's Christians stunned, repentant, and determined to change their ways.

Today it is governments that are slaying people who follow religions deemed to be enemies. It was the government in El Salvador that killed Archbishop Oscar Romero, six Jesuit professors, and four American churchwomen. It was the governments in Berlin, Moscow, and Beijing that killed countless persons of faith deemed to be the enemies of the state.

Can more treaties and more emphasis on the necessity of religious freedom change the dreadful pattern that has historically been followed? The framers of the United Nations Declaration on Religious Freedom and all the most idealistic and humanitarian persons since the end of World War II have placed their confidence in the rule of law, the inviolability of human rights, and the exaltation of religious freedom as the best ways to restore and preserve civilization. Their words have been translated into world law binding on all 191 member states of the United Nations. The governments of these countries have made solemn pledges to enforce those moral concepts in their own laws.

One of the most urgent of all those objectives, the advancement of religious freedom, has received disappointingly little attention by the UN's member states and even by the religious bodies it was designed to protect. History may well record that one of the greatest disappointments in the second half of the twentieth century was the neglect and the silence that governments and religious organizations extended to the efforts of the United Nations to preserve and enlarge religious freedom.

Of course, many religious groups have actively sought to guarantee religious freedom to everyone in the world. One example is the Parliament of World Religions, held in August 1993, which brought 6,500 individuals to Chicago from fifty-six nations and from nearly all the world's major religions. The parliament's "Declaration Towards a Global Ethic" echoed the sentiments of the first World Parliament of Religion, held in Chicago in 1893.

The final statement in the parliament's declaration is not expressly theistic, but rather embraces concepts of human dignity that are applicable to a wide range of beliefs. Its statement on the Golden Rule is as follows: "There is a principle which is found and has persisted in many religious and ethical traditions of human kind for thousands of years: What you do not wish done to yourself, do not do to others! Or in positive terms: What you wish done to yourself, do to others! This should be the irrevocable, unconditional norm for all areas of life, for families and communities, for races, nations and religions."

Some people may feel that this statement is too general to be particularly helpful in efforts to resolve awful dilemmas surrounded by agonizing problems. But at least it is a global effort to bring religious personages of all backgrounds together and make a pledge to live by the Golden Rule.

Will there ever be an age when God and Caesar can co-exist in peace? Law is a feeble instrument to bring about that laudable objective. If law is to be effective, it must be joined with love—and love for others is at the core of every religion and every code of conduct. There is no simple way to summarize the meaning and enormous consequences of love for every human being, but St. John does it as well as anyone: "Let us love one another, for love comes from God. Whoever loves is a child of God and knows God. Whoever does not love does not know God, because God is love" (1 John 4:7–8).

Appendix A
United Nations Declaration on the Elimination of All Forms of Intolerance and of Discrimination Based on Religion or Belief (1981)

The General Assembly,

Considering that one of the basic principles of the Charter of the United Nations is that of the dignity and equality inherent in all human beings, and that all Member States have pledged themselves to take joint and separate action in co-operation with the United Nations to promote and encourage universal respect for and observance of human rights and fundamental freedoms for all, without distinction as to race, sex, language or religion,

Considering that the Universal Declaration of Human Rights and the International Covenants on Human Rights proclaim the principles of non-discrimination and equality before the law and the right to freedom of thought, conscience, religion or belief,

Considering that the disregard and infringement of human rights and fundamental freedoms, in particular of the right to freedom of thought, conscience, religion or whatever belief, have brought, directly or indirectly, wars and great suffering to mankind, especially where they serve as a means of foreign interference in the internal affairs of other States, and amount to kindling hatred between peoples and nations,

G.A. Res. 36/55 of Nov. 25, 1981, U.N. GAOR, 36th Sess., Supp. No. 51, 73d plen. mtg. at 171, U.N. Doc. A/36/51 (1982), reprinted in 21 I.L.M. 205 (1982).

Considering that religion or belief, for anyone who professes either, is one of the fundamental elements in his conception of life and that freedom of religion or belief should be fully respected and guaranteed,

Considering that it is essential to promote understanding, tolerance and respect in matters relating to freedom of religion or belief and to ensure that the use of religion or belief for ends inconsistent with the Charter, other relevant instruments of the United Nations and the purposes and principles of the present Declaration is inadmissible,

Convinced that freedom of religion or belief should also contribute to the attainment of the goals of world peace, social justice and friendship among peoples and to the elimination of ideologies or practices of colonialism and racial discrimination,

Noting with satisfaction the adoption of several, and the coming into force of some, conventions, under the aegis of the United Nations and of the specialized agencies, for the elimination of various forms of discrimination,

Concerned by manifestations of intolerance and by the existence of discrimination in matters of religion or belief still in evidence in some areas of the world,

Resolved to adopt all necessary measures for the speedy elimination of such intolerance in all its forms and manifestations and to prevent and to combat discrimination on the grounds of religion or belief,

Proclaims this Declaration on the Elimination of All Forms of Intolerance and of Discrimination Based on Religion or Belief:

Article 1

1. Everyone shall have the right to freedom of thought, conscience and religion. This right shall include freedom to have a religion or whatever belief of his choice, and freedom, either individually or in community with others and in public or private, to manifest his religion or belief in worship, observance, practice and teaching.

2. No one shall be subject to coercion which would impair his freedom to have a religion or belief of his choice.

3. Freedom to manifest one's religion or belief may be subject only to such limitations as are prescribed by law and are necessary to protect public safety, order, health or morals or the fundamental rights and freedoms of others.

Article 2

1. No one shall be subject to discrimination by any State, institution, group of persons or person on the grounds of religion or belief.
2. For the purposes of the present Declaration, the expression "intolerance and discrimination based on religion or belief" means any distinction, exclusion, restriction or preference based on religion or belief and having as its purpose or as its effect nullification or impairment of the recognition, enjoyment or exercise of human rights and fundamental freedoms on an equal basis.

Article 3

Discrimination between human beings on the grounds of religion or belief constitutes an affront to human dignity and a disavowal of the principles of the Charter of the United Nations, and shall be condemned as a violation of the human rights and fundamental freedoms proclaimed in the Universal Declaration of Human Rights and enunciated in detail in the International Covenants on Human Rights, and as an obstacle to friendly and peaceful relations between nations.

Article 4

1. All States shall take effective measures to prevent and eliminate discrimination on the grounds of religion or belief in the recognition, exercise and enjoyment of human rights and fundamental freedoms in all fields of civil, economic, political, social and cultural life.
2. All States shall make all efforts to enact or rescind legislation where necessary to prohibit any such discrimination, and to take all appropriate measures to combat intolerance on the grounds of religion or belief in this matter.

Article 5

1. The parents or, as the case may be, the legal guardians of the child have the right to organize the life within the family in

accordance with their religion or belief and bearing in mind the moral education in which they believe the child should be brought up.

2. Every child shall enjoy the right to have access to education in the matter of religion or belief in accordance with the wishes of his parents or, as the case may be, legal guardians, and shall not be compelled to receive teaching on religion or belief against the wishes of his parents or legal guardians, the best interests of the child being the guiding principle.

3. The child shall be protected from any form of discrimination on the grounds of religion or belief. He shall be brought up in a spirit of understanding, tolerance, friendship among peoples, peace and universal brotherhood, respect for freedom of religion or belief of others, and in full consciousness that his energy and talents should be devoted to the service of his fellow men.

4. In the case of a child who is not under the care either of his parents or of legal guardians, due account shall be taken of either expressed wishes or of any other proof of their wishes in the matter of religion or belief, the best interests of the child being the guiding principle.

5. Practices of a religion or belief in which a child is brought up must not be injurious to his physical or mental health or to his full development, taking into account Article 1, paragraph 3, of the present Declaration.

Article 6

In accordance with Article 1 of the present Declaration, and subject to the provisions of Article 1, paragraph 3, the right to freedom of thought, conscience, religion or belief shall include, *inter alia*, the following freedoms:

(a) To worship or assemble in connection with a religion or belief, and to establish and maintain places for these purposes;

(b) To establish and maintain appropriate charitable or humanitarian institutions;

(c) To make, acquire and use to an adequate extent the necessary articles and materials related to the rites or customs of a religion or belief;

(d) To write, issue and disseminate relevant publications in these areas;

(e) To teach a religion or belief in places suitable for these purposes;

(f) To solicit and receive voluntary financial and other contributions from individuals and institutions;

(g) To train, appoint, elect or designate by succession appropriate leaders called for by the requirements and standards of any religion or belief;

(h) To observe days of rest and to celebrate holidays and ceremonies in accordance with the precepts of one's religion or belief;

(i) To establish and maintain communications with individuals and communities in matters of religion or belief at the national and international levels.

Article 7

The rights and freedoms set forth in the present Declaration shall be accorded in national legislations in such a manner that everyone shall be able to avail himself of such rights and freedoms in practice.

Article 8

Nothing in the present Declaration shall be construed as restricting or derogating from any right defined in the Universal Declaration of Human Rights and the International Covenant on Human Rights.

Appendix B
Vatican II Statement on the Jews

As this Sacred Synod probes the mystery of the Church, it remembers the spiritual bond that ties the people of the New Covenant to Abraham's stock.

Thus the Church of Christ acknowledges that, according to God's saving design, the beginnings of her faith and election go back as far as the days of the patriarchs, of Moses, and of the prophets. She affirms that all who believe in Christ—Abraham's sons according to the faith (cf. Gal. 3:7)—are included in the call of this patriarch; she also affirms that her salvation is mysteriously prefigured in the exodus of the chosen people from the land of bondage. The Church, therefore, cannot forget that she received the revelation of the Old Testament through the people with whom God, in that loving kindness words cannot express, deigned to conclude the Ancient Covenant. Nor can she forget that she draws sustenance from the root of that well-cultivated olive tree onto which the wild roots of the Gentiles have been grafted (Rom. 11:17–24). For the Church believes that by His cross Christ, who is our Peace, reconciled Jews and Gentiles, making the two one in Himself (cf. Eph. 2:14–16).

The Church keeps ever before her eyes the words of the Apostle about his kinsmen: "There is the sonship and the glory and the covenants and the law and the worship and the promises; theirs are the patriarchs and from them is the Christ according to the flesh" (Rom. 9:4–5), the Son of the Virgin Mary. Furthermore, she recalls that the apostles, the Church's foundation-stones and pillars (cf. Ap. 21:14, Gal. 2:9), sprang from the Jewish people, as did most of the early disciples who proclaimed Christ's Gospel to the world.

As Holy Scripture testifies, Jerusalem did not recognize the time of her visitation (cf. Lk. 19:44), nor did the Jews in large number accept the

Gospel; indeed, not a few opposed its dissemination (cf. Rom. 11:28). Nevertheless, now as before, God holds them most dear, for the sake of the patriarchs; He has not withdrawn His gifts or calling—such is the witness of the Apostle (Rom. 11:28–29). In company with the prophets and the same Apostle, the Church awaits that day, known to God alone, on which all peoples will address the Lord in a single voice and "serve him with one accord" (Soph. 3:9; cf. Is. 66:23; Ps. 66[65]:4; Rom. 11:11–32).

Since the spiritual patrimony common to Christians and Jews is so rich, this Sacred Synod wishes to encourage and further their mutual knowledge of, and respect for, one another, a knowledge and respect born principally of biblical and theological studies, but also of fraternal dialogue.

True, the Jewish authorities and those who sided with them pressed for the death of Christ (cf. Jn. 19:6); still, what happened in His passion cannot be attributed without distinction to all Jews then alive, nor can it be attributed to the Jews of today. Certainly, the Church is the new people of God; nevertheless, the Jews are not to be presented as rejected or accursed by God, as if this followed them from Holy Scripture. May all, then, see to it that nothing is taught, either in catechetical work or in the preaching of the word of God, that does not conform to the truth of the Gospel and the spirit of Christ.

The Church, moreover, rejects any persecution against any man. For this reason and for the sake of her common patrimony with the Jews, she decries hatred, persecutions, displays of anti-Semitism, staged against the Jews at whatever time in history and by whomsoever. She does so, not moved by political reasons, but impelled by the Gospel's pure love.

One thing remains: Christ underwent His passion and death freely and out of infinite love because of the sins of all men so that all may obtain salvation. This the Church has always held and holds now. Sent to preach, the Church is, therefore, bound to proclaim the cross of Christ as the sign of God's all-embracing love and as the fountain from which every grace flows.

Selected Bibliography

Blackburn, Robert, and Jörg Polakiewicz, eds. *Fundamental Rights in Europe: The European Convention on Human Rights and Its Member States, 1950–2000.* Oxford: Oxford University Press, 2001.

Boyle, Kevin, and Juliet Sheen. *Freedom of Religion and Belief: A World Report.* London: Routledge, 1997.

Cumper, Peter, and Steven Wheatley, eds. *Minority Rights in the "New" Europe.* The Hague: Martinus Nijhoff, 1999.

Dunne, Tim, and Nicholas J. Wheeler, eds. *Human Rights in Global Politics.* Cambridge: Cambridge University Press, 1999.

Evans, Carolyn. *Freedom of Religion under the European Convention on Human Rights.* Oxford: Oxford University Press, 2001.

Falk, Richard. *Religion and Humane Global Governance.* New York: Palgrave, 2001.

Foot, Rosemary. *Rights beyond Borders: The Global Community and the Struggle over Human Rights in China.* Oxford: Oxford University Press, 2000.

Hammer, Leonard M. *The International Human Right to Freedom of Conscience: Some Suggestions for Its Development and Application.* Burlington, Vt.: Ashgate, 2001.

Howland, Courtney W., ed. *Religious Fundamentalism and the Human Rights of Women.* New York: St. Martin's Press, 1999.

Janis, Mark W., and Carolyn W. Evans, eds. *Religion and International Law.* The Hague: Martinus Nijhoff, 1999.

Johnston, Douglas, and Cynthia Sampson, eds. *Religion, the Missing Dimension of Statecraft.* Oxford: Oxford University Press, 1994.

Lerner, Natan. *Religion, Beliefs, and International Human Rights.* Maryknoll, N.Y.: Orbis Books, 2000.

Mayer, Ann Elizabeth. *Islam and Human Rights: Tradition and Politics.* 2nd ed. Boulder, Colo.: Westview, 1995.

Sigmund, Paul E., ed. *Religious Freedom and Evangelization in Latin America: The Challenge of Religious Pluralism.* Maryknoll, N.Y.: Orbis Books, 1999.

Tahzib, Bahiyyih G. *Freedom of Religion or Belief: Ensuring Effective International Legal Protection.* The Hague: Martinus Nijhoff, 1996.

Traer, Robert. *Faith in Human Rights: Support in Religious Traditions for a Global Struggle.* Washington, D.C.: Georgetown University Press, 1991.

Van der Vyver, Johan D., and John Witte Jr., eds. *Religious Human Rights in Global Perspective: Legal Perspectives.* The Hague: Martinus Nijhoff, 1996.

Whitte, John Jr., and Johan D. van der Vyver, eds. *Religious Human Rights in Global Perspective: Religious Perspectives.* The Hague: Martin Nijhoff, 1996.

Index